The Healing Muse

Muse

A Journal of Literary and Visual Arts

The Healing Muse is SUNY Upstate Medical University's journal of literary and visual arts published annually by the Center for Bioethics and Humanities.

The Center for Bioethics and Humanities at SUNY Upstate, established through the generous support of the Medical Alumni Association, is committed to promoting health care which is patient-centered, compassionate, and just. We accomplish this through educational initiatives in bioethics and the medical humanities, clinical ethics consultation, multidisciplinary research and scholarly writing, and health policy analysis and advocacy.

Cover art: *Fiume Arno, Italia* by Yolanda Tooley

©2011 SUNY Upstate Medical University

ISSN 1539-6983

ISBN 978-0-9789605-5-1

The Healing Muse

A Journal of Literary and Visual Arts

ℬ ℬ ℬ

Table of Contents

Poetry

Non-Fiction

Fiction

Visuals

Editor's Note

This is a book about distance, a fitting concept for a journal devoted to notions and images of healing. The writers and artists in these pages have traveled and crossed wide and disparate distances to reach a place or a measure of acceptance.

We began *The Healing Muse* to encourage a dialogue among all those engaged in healing: clinicians, patients, caregivers, and friends. Each year we are humbled by the stories sent to us and delighted by the artistry used to convey them. While suffering is as old as humanity, its manifestation can be unique to each age. Our age knows the ravages of cancer, and indeed, in this issue many of our writers meet the challenge of telling the all too familiar tale of its arrival in new and affecting ways.

Illness doesn't just alter the patient's life; it causes shifts and upheavals in families and friends, in work routines and personal expectations. In this issue, we meet people struggling and coping with the after effects of electric shock treatments, amniocentesis results, drug dependency, and the death of a loved one. Sometimes they write about their own experiences; sometimes they describe another's, but in every case they craft an indelible phrase, a unique image that brings the reader as close as possible to what it felt like to hear that diagnosis or live that prognosis. The courage, the wit, and the passion they record linger in the reader's mind and heart linking us in ways social media can only envy.

I chose "Distance," one of B.A. St. Andrews's unpublished poems, to open this issue; eight years after her death, her words remind us that language allows the impossible: "I throw my heart / As if it were a hawk, / into the sky / and bid it fly to you." Strong hearts beat throughout this issue bearing witness to love and faith, to people dedicated to shepherding loved ones through procedures and side effects, through altered bodies and weary minds. In the poem, the speaker's heart lands "harmless as a rainbow, / a wish, an autumn leaf / on your outstretched hand." This image we offer to our readers, in much the same fashion those engaged in healing offer their loved ones and patients.

With such love and confidence we bridge these distances between life as it was and life as it is now.

Deirdre Neilen
Vol. 11, No. 1 (Fall) 2011

Founding Editor

B.A. St. Andrews
(1945-2003)

Distance

B.A. St. Andrews

Across the mountains
your heart sleeps.

This love that tears
my breast can find

no rest inside the mews.
I throw my heart

As if it were a hawk,
into the sky

and bid it fly to you.
Fierce and fleet

its wings beat against
this separating air

to accomplish what it
cannot understand.

Believe that it will
land harmless as a rainbow,

a wish, an autumn leaf
on your outstretched hand.

Cover Artist

I embraced black & white film photography over twenty-five years ago and have never tired of its multifaceted and magical qualities. I sometimes hand color the prints to give them a different air, collage them to express complex ideas, solarize to intensify a dark mood and mood is what drew me in the first place—monochromatic images emanate powerful vibrations. Like a musical score, listen to my photographs, they will sing for you.

Yolanda Tooley 2011

Yolanda Tooley ~ *Street Music 2*

Kathleen Gunton ~ *Beyond Obstacles*

Poetry and Grace

Bruce Bennett

Poetry is not grace;
it can't absolve
a sinner, or replace
lost faith, or solve

Conundrums by what's learned
beyond the grave.
But it is swift, unearned,
and it can save.

Dark and Bright

Bruce Bennett

The dark side of a blessing.
The bright side of a curse.
The substance of what's missing.
The best in what was worse

Through loss that keeps on giving
and light that gilds despair.
This life beyond that living.
That gift that's always there.

I Killed a Man with My Own Two Hands

Amy L. Friedman
Dearing Writing Award, Prose
Faculty/Employee Division

I killed a man with my two hands. I didn't mean to. It was an error—an error made by a human being. I am the human who made that error. This error—my error, cost him his life. When his life ended, mine changed forever. I am trying to survive.

I had given this man my oath to honor his trust in me and in my judgment, in my ability to make the system work on his behalf, in my guarantee to be transparent about the known and unknown as it transpired in his care, and in my promise to skillfully repair his broken anatomy. We had peered into each other's unclothed souls while he held the hand I purposefully offered in confident closure of my pledge. Today, I still desperately need to believe my long ago promise was offered out of conviction, not arrogance. But this only matters to me, since nothing can change the outcome. I had been wrong. My hands were not good enough on that day. My promise was broken because I broke it.

The moment his vein slipped from my fingers I knew he had died, though we worked for another sixty-eight minutes. The problem I had created simply had no solution. Even now, so many years later, as I once again feel the diaphanous, blue tissue escape, my heart is suddenly racing, my breaths are rapid and shallow, and I can only clearly see these words on the page while everything else has become blurred and sounds have become far away, much like those first seconds when his blood began welling up. Flashbacks don't come as often these days, but are no less awful when they do. We have probably all wondered how horrible it must have been for the Titanic victims to have foreseen their own drowning deaths in the freezing ocean waters, or for the Challenger astronauts to have known they were falling impossible miles to earth within their intact, yet doomed, capsule. At least the pain and suffering did end for those poor souls. When my fingers failed to control this man's vessel, I knew instantly that death would happen with that same certainty. And it did. But it was his death, not my own. Fortunately, he did not suffer or have pain because he was appropriately prepared. But others did. And I am one of them. How might one measure whether it is more awful to bear the knowledge of imminent death if it is your own, or it is a death you have caused and must continue trying to personally survive, or why? Regrettably, this was such a moment of inevitability, and it was terrible. But for me it did not stop with his death, because I replay it over and over again. Can I ever give it back? Please? Such knowledge simply escapes description. For a long time, perishing with this man was very inviting. Continued existence did not seem possible.

When time slowed, the faces and voices around me blurred and my team watched every move as I reached deep into the virtual bag of tricks that I already knew to be empty, in contrast to Mary Poppins' magic carpetbag. Would my colleagues immediately accept that there was no answer in my bag and that we could simply stop our efforts right then? Such a judgment would have seemed so brash, and inappropriate, and ultimately have led to such severe consequences from those unable to grasp the key surgical issues that I chose to continue what I knew to be a charade, even though expensive and valuable resources were expended in doing so. To save face and to avoid answering difficult questions, I stood there hopelessly prolonging the bloodbath. Was my choice wrong or weak or simply practical? To this day, it still seems like the best one to have made, because it allowed my teammates to feel as if they had personally tried desperately to save his life. I cared about them, and do not regret having done so. If I was cowardly in choosing the more traveled road, and being self-protective, forgive me. On this charge, just this one, I have fully forgiven myself.

After thanking everyone for their help, I dragged myself to the scrub sink outside the bloody operating room and saw the stool and clean scrubs my circulating nurse had prepared for me. She knew just how drained I was, how much paperwork and other responsibilities still awaited my attention, and how hard it would be for me to face his family. She gifted me with those two simple acts of kindness and caring at a very tough time. To this day they remain the only words or actions acknowledging that death's impact on me that I have ever received from any member of a healthcare system. I will always be grateful for her thoughtfulness.

I had to tell his wife. She was devastated, as one would expect. I had to tell my husband. He was supportive, as one would hope. I continue to find solace from my spouse. The man's spouse cannot say the same. On that night I was inconsolable. I remember the warm bath water my husband used to soothe my shaking limbs, the calming words he spoke, the softness of the cloth on my face, and the way he cradled me to his chest. I could never bear to think about how she made it through that night.

But at work no one ever said a personal word about his death. Most would not look directly at me—or maybe that was just my perception. Without pause, I resumed operating. The case was reviewed through the usual processes. In today's terminology, it resulted from a human error, not a system error. No checklist or timeout could have prevented the death. At the time, I could not speak about the details of the case with anyone else, because our conversation would have been discoverable. No grief counselor was offered. I could not share my grief. I worried about being sued yet no legal advice was offered. Ultimately, I survived the statute of limitations. That provided a certain type of relief.

His death was shocking, though I am very comfortable with deaths from patient disease, even those occurring intra-operatively. But, this was death caused by me making a technical error that another surgeon might not have made. On that day, I was not a good enough surgeon—a mighty big thorn. Had I been wrong in believing I could safely perform such a procedure? Before his case, I had done so for other patients. After his death, I always feared that very step in each of the cases that unfolded exactly as planned, even with subsequent patients doing well. I always thought of him as my fingers held their tissues tight. But in his case, it was an irretrievable error. I can never forgive myself for that error. Somehow, completely on my own, I needed to understand how to tolerate being imperfect.

We surgeons do not offer each other much comfort or compassion. No department, or hospital or legal group has ever openly arranged for team support that has been apparent to me. Neither have I have ever known another surgeon to candidly seek such solace. Perhaps they do, and I don't know it. But, why should I not know? Is that appropriate? If I have suffered so greatly in carrying this load, can I truly be alone in such personal sorrow? Surely I am not the only imperfect surgeon, or the only human one. Am I unusually sensitive or insufficiently inured to my own shortcomings? At last, now, I find relief in sharing with you that I still care about a man whom I killed so long ago. It has been an awful secret. Not his death, because that was never hidden. But my response and grief that were so tightly contained, and the disappointment I have in myself. I was provided no outlet for my tears. Surgeons are expected to appear strong and poised. The reality is that I still cry for him. I am crying now.

I killed a man with my two hands. I am only a human being. Part of me died on that day too.

From the Motel Window

Amy Haddad

Brake lights bleed on the gray snow
as cars and buses move in and out
of the teeming parking lot. Healthy and young,
students and coaches trudge to the stadium entrance,
a swim meet, the sign says. Their breath hangs
in misty clouds over their heads.

She stares down from the motel window,
while the tiny phone delivers crushing news.
Every detail of the scene below is burned
in her mind. She hears the words, all bad,
"tests inconclusive," "multi-system failure,"
"may not survive the night," but her attention
is on the dirty snow, the cold she cannot feel,
and the silence in the room. She pulls
the curtains behind her and leans closer
to the window looking down, trying to listen.

The grave voice on the phone
asks about next steps. She knows there are none
merely laying the groundwork for death.
She is trapped here, not where she should be.

Forever she will think this is what grief
looks like, frozen on the other side of a transparent
wall where you can see others move and breathe
but you cannot hear what they say or feel
the cold on your face and in your throat.

February Second

Barbara Crooker

The lines in italics are from An Exact Replica of a Figment of my Imagination
by Elizabeth McCracken
A child dies in this book. . . .a baby is stillborn.

The snow is coming down again, the ground pale as Snow White's skin,
and a blood-red cardinal lands on the black lid of the barbecue,
where I've scattered some seeds. In the book I'm reading, a sentence
flies off the page, flaps between my eyes: *It's a happy life, but someone
is missing.* Someone is always missing. Time stopped forty years ago
in the delivery room in those last moments before the nurse
couldn't find the heartbeat. I became a watch that no longer ticks.
You cannot change time, but I wish I could be innocent again,
believing all stories have happy endings. *Closure is bullshit.*
You never forget, though everyone else does. Here is a birthday
unmarked on a calendar, where no cake is baked, no icing piles up
in drifts, no candles are wished on. Forever after, I am the bad fairy,
the one you don't want to invite to the christening. This story is
so sad that no one remembers it, and I have to tell it again and again.
Just like this snow, which keeps stuttering down, trying to write
its little white lies, but the black facts refuse to be swaddled;
their harsh calls rise up, crows on the snow.

Etiquette for the Very Ill

Johanna Shapiro

Let's say you get cancer
or have a heart attack
or get hit by a bus
You may think you need a doctor
or a hospital
But what you really need
is a lesson in etiquette
Otherwise you will end up
making a very bad impression
on friends, family,
doctors, nurses,
and complete strangers
so that
while struggling to live
or struggling to die
you will also be universally perceived
as completely lacking
in decorum

Etiquette
That's right

By getting so sick
you've just committed
a serious social faux pas
That's French for
a fucking bad mistake
from which you will probably
never recover
Ha-ha
(Generally speaking,
as a very sick person,
you want to avoid mordant humor

But what's a joke or two
among friends?)

Believe me,
when you are a very sick person
you need etiquette

Lesson #1
It is a good idea
when you are desperately ill
to know a little French
French is a classy language
and as a very ill person,
it will give you a certain
je ne sais quoi
(That's French too
Look it up)
If you do not already
know French
you will have plenty of time
to learn it
in doctors' waiting rooms

Lesson #2
When you become
a very ill person
it is most important
that you avoid self-pity
This is a very disagreeable emotion
to others
Also anger, despair, misery (especially
the wallowing kind) are bad
Bitter is very bad
When you show these emotions
you make healthy people
feel guilty and uncomfortable
Healthy people can be unkind
They have plenty of energy

Lesson #3
As you might imagine,
smiling is never out of place
If you aren't very ill yet
try smiling as you stick a
needle (an ordinary sewing needle is fine)

under your fingernail
You can add "thank you" later

If you allow yourself to become
a very ill person who behaves badly
then it will end very badly for you
because everyone will despise you
for having atrocious manners
On the other hand,
it will probably end very badly for you
anyway.

Susannah Loiselle ~ *Broken Down*

Waiting Room

Elizabeth W. Carey
Dearing Writing Award, Prose
Faculty/Employee Division

One time between 1997 - 2001

My dad said, "If I had my way, I would know it was time to go, and would push off on an ice flow like an old Eskimo, without bother or burden." With little fanfare or hoopla, my dad wanted to go efficiently and quietly. We do not live near any ice flows, let alone an expansive ocean vast enough to allow for drifting away or floating over the horizon undisturbed.

September 2007

Drizzle, unabated condensation characteristic of most days that year in Portland, coated us in an instant. In the seconds it took to rush from the back porch to the gravel driveway, where my father sat warming up the car, one gloved hand on the wheel and the other on the stick already in reverse, moisture met skin and Gortex. Billions of droplets coated my mom's hair, making brown and gray almost iridescent under the low dome light.

I ran a few minutes behind—my tardiness measured on the family clock. To arrive at least fifteen minutes prior to the scheduled appointment time, my dad would occasionally drive himself; three people would take two cars ten miles north, skirting the Willamette River through the city, to Kaiser's Interstate oncology facility.

I had to eat on the way—something or anything—because we were not sure what the doctor would say. And as Phoebe knew, low blood sugar or not, I could start seeing spots across my vision when she'd review size of bone mets or implications of blood counts. I feared fainting in those rooms, especially because I was not the patient. How embarrassing to look up at overworked nurses tending to me, just dizzy. That's why I would have to focus on breathing, remembering to take each inhale fully, and pull up my sleeves, especially if she OK'd chemo and we'd walk Dad to the injection room.

Down into the concrete parking structure we drove, to park on the purple or orange level. Rain puddled along the open side of the building. To enter, I pushed the handicap button to open the automatic door; Dad pushed the revolving door for himself and Mom and, once inside, would shake off his slicker, handing his satchel to Mom while he got out his card. Smells from a Sysco-supplied cafeteria wafted up the atrium. Few voices rose.

We walked to the double glass doors, propped open by the last person in line. Dad took his place. Mom and I made our way through the seating area, careful to avoid the hard-backed pink loveseat that hurt Dad's hips, looking for three empty seats clumped together. I took the sliding rocker, the kind that would make his vertigo go, near the puzzle table, in between two low armchairs covered in faded florals. It was not difficult to tell who the patients were. Many were waiting, and about half looked ashen, pale, yellow with bloodshot eyes.

Most eyes, even the receptionists', looked tired. Dad's were puffy, like all Careys' including my own. But his twinkled that morning when he told me about his walk. Unable to sleep from 3:30 am on, he got up at 6 and made it down to the railroad tracks, which he followed to Spokane Avenue, past the little white chapel. Not quite to the park or Monkey Trails from Oaks Bottom Wildlife Refuge up to the Doug Fir-lined cliff, but more than he'd done in awhile, at least since the pain in his bones spread.

October 29, 1997

Outside Sellwood Middle School, on SE 15th Street, he idled. I'd been called out of class and excused for the day. After I buckled up in Bon Mot, the first of his white Corollas, we drove north to the bridge, then south to Lake Oswego.

My dad picked me up because Grandpa died. Then he cried. I'd never seen his face scrunch up like that or watched him wipe tears away from behind black wire bifocals.

We rode then, quietly—the two of us knowing how miserable Grandpa Joe had been with cancer, how sober for nine years, how crazed with anesthesia, how fascinated with clouds and planes and photography and the Wars and the Orient. And how he enjoyed shooting squirrels with his BB gun and feeding humming-birds with red sugar water. I thought about how he loved all jellybeans except the black licorice ones, all two grandkids except when they shrieked.

"He's not feeling pain anymore," my dad said.

Any time after October 2002

Planning for any trip is interrupted by appointments, pharmacy runs, phone calls, doctor emails, researching experimental studies, tattoo-markers, chemo needles and, oh, pain: the pain of inactivity; the hurt of sitting. This pain melts glaciers, shrinks icebergs, stops snow and brings out the bright, bright sun to shine on our vision of the land of the Eskimos: no running, no biking, no motorcycle riding, no driving, and, then, no walking. This light casts no shadows—just reveals a rock hard landscape.

Out here, the enemy is predatory and elusive, if definable. It is not the cougar that stalked Dad on his antelope hunt, the one who left paw prints in the snow larger than Dad's outstretched hand around the one-man tent pitched on Central Oregon's high desert plains. But it is after meat and bones. It waits, stalks, surges forth, slinks back, attacks, and then sits on its haunches, hunting the hunter with no map or compass or track.

Its pervasive presence shape shifts everywhere. I see it in family, friends' families, at clinics, in the infusion room, on the street; in those hairless or jaundiced or toothless or scarred or perfectly normal except for hallowed out eyes. I see its shifty iterations in every body tagged with a LIVESTRONG band. We, with those plastic yellow wristbands, are on alert. Watching for the formidable enemy, we count the days we are active one at a time.

Noon, May 15, 2006

The original prognosis, delivered during the fall of my freshman year of college, did not provide sufficient time for my dad to make it to my graduation. I attended the college he said we ought not go into debt for, the college about which he eventually became enthused, once he realized how many of its professors were interviewed on NPR and even in *The Financial Times*.

He continued to live with austerity and discipline. Determined enough, he made it to and through my commencement ceremony on this day in New York City. Here, in the most earnest and sincere of moments, he tells me he is proud of my BA in the Big Apple. He sees what I love-hate about Manhattan, the Ivy League, the world; and he sees I no longer hate him and maybe he can some day say he loves me.

October 2008

In the waiting room, the things that make me queasy are not the same that make me lightheaded in the patient exam rooms. From the sliding rocker, I face the one glass wall of the room, so I can see people coming and going and stay focused on the business of the world as it revolves around the sun, or whatever is going on outside this stuffy, overheated, and hushed place. It is lowly-lit, ill-designed, dimly-fashioned, except for the kids' play corner.

There, primary colors are scattered like splashes of paint. Elsewhere, some yarn stuffed in and overflowing from quilting bags with narrow circular knitting needles assists in illumination. I see doctors in scrubs and administrators in suits walk past. Dad, to my left, wears a cotton tee shirt and unbuttoned flannel, a Pendleton. Mom, to my right, is still in her black and white plaid rain jacket, which glitters with a bit of remnant mist.

I think there is nothing fair about the weather today or ever in this gray climate, and most certainly nothing (nothing!) sensical about the parade of people hurrying in to line up, to check in, to sit, to wait, to listen, and to watch, then to be called, then to wait again, squinting under fluorescent lights, to find out if chemo is even worth it. My stomach turns.

A tall man in an M's baseball hat stoops to reach the handlebars of a wheelchair. He pushes a woman through the doors and her youth startles me, but not as much as her burgeoning belly. She is at once pregnant and yellow. A white towel wrap covers her head where hair should be. There is nothing bittersweet about her; it is all sour and sad. There is no room in her tired, tired eyes for color, let alone hope.

I feel miserable. For I get sad when I think Dad won't walk me down an aisle; that the mets are growing and PSA rises incrementally; and that he has trouble getting into the car. But at least (at least!) I have this: he knows me. I feel my heart break in my chest and fall to my stomach at the same time. I want to vomit.

Midmorning, June 6, 2009

My father, an atheist, penciled future activities in his slim black monthly planner religiously. But the day he knew would come did so on its own time. The transfusions hinted at its arrival, as did his changing demeanor. But no one tells you what to look for when someone's dying, and it sure as hell does not happen like the euphemisms people use.

Thank god for the straight-shooting hospice nurse. With her black bob motionless atop her petite, plump frame, she put it to me. The force of her words pushed me back against the fridge and I slumped to the floor. She put it to us, my mom and me, to be the ones to care for him; to help him go; to let him be; to push his ice flow into a cold, dark sea, to leave this wretched world and beautiful compassion and all the flighty antelope and sneaky cougars behind.

Activity flurried and waned. We'd practiced for years. We knew how to hurry up (learn med doses and bedside care and make calls after deciding who to call) and wait (sit. make tea. sit. then get up and not know what to say. so for one of the first times be numb enough for unplanned, prolonged silence. and in our home we made room for new sounds: his speech, slurred, and breathing, both heavy and raspy). And again we hurried and waited. This time was for real, for love, for family. We watched our loss unfurl.

The Night Before Surgery

Joan Cofrancesco
Dearing Writing Award, Poetry
Faculty/Employee Division

The sorrow of an old horse in a pasture
Never running again. The plane that crashed into the towers
holds darkness in its wings for eternity.

Each time Van Gogh touches his brush to the page
so many sunflowers and irises light up. Perhaps that happens
because we have caused so much darkness.

Each time a surgeon cuts through my skin
I hope he is like Van Gogh with a brush
though I know the universe can get along without me.

Our bodies seem to remember our suffering
Our hearts seem to clog like rusty drains
Our souls remember all those smoky bars.

Last night I dreamt of
Galloping beasts and dripping colors.
I was running in a field with a horse
no cares no suffering.

How could it be that such suffering
Could be shown by a sketch of
Black crows flying through a dark cornfield?

Orthopedic Surgery

Joan Cofrancesco

At the hospital in that rouge of light
of 9 or 10 morphine shots, you could pass
for the white rabbit; we could hop all night
down the white halls and through that looking glass
in flying shining slippers. As Alice
my body grows larger as we dine,
your white tail bops nervously through a kiss.
I grow intelligent about my spine.
But this high life is trying; Cheshire cats
take us from the table; hand in white paw
we seek more thrills—a madman in a blue cap
OR tables and crazy queens with saws.
In this land I'd rather stay in my hole
Than risk my back being turned into a steel pole.

Haiku

Joan Cofrancesco

stretchers—white boats pass-
ing each other in blue halls—
and the earth is flat

Kathleen Gunton ~ *Choices*

Apartment 5B

Antara B. Mitra
Dearing Writing Award, Prose
Student Division

Maya scanned through the matrimonial classifieds in the Sunday newspaper to find her ad. It was a sea of newsprint that required a magnifying glass to view. The city was teeming with young men and women looking to find mates.

"Are you sure they printed it?" Maya asked her mother who sat beside her in a wicker chair.

"Oh, give me that." Mrs. Chopra leaned forward and snatched the newspaper, the chair creaking ominously under her shifting weight. "It's right here, in the center." She jabbed a stout finger at the newspaper.

> Homely girl, 22 years, college graduate, works in local dance school.
> Can cook, sew and knit. Only child. Pleasant temperament.

Maya peered at the classified, creasing her forehead as she read.

"Don't frown, nobody will marry you," Mrs. Chopra said.

"Homely! Nobody will marry me now in any case," Maya wailed.

Maya and her mother, Mrs. Chopra, lived in apartment 5B of a modest apartment building, imaginatively named Paradise Apartments, in a middle class neighborhood of Delhi. It was one of many in that particular area, where the government had earmarked land for the construction of residential high rises to alleviate the housing crunch in the capital. The result was a crop of buildings, thick and plentiful, like mushrooms growing in a dank forest. The buildings were large monolithic structures, distinguished only by superficial architectural details like arched doorways or neoclassical columns. They were built to maximize the number of units in each building while keeping costs to a minimum. There was no relief from the grey of the buildings to the grey of the streets, crowded with the teeming thousands who lived here.

Until a few months ago, apartment 5B had also been the abode of Mr. Chopra, who had succumbed to a long-standing heart ailment brought on by smoking and his favorite evening snack—deep fried pakoras. On the death of her husband, Mrs. Chopra proclaimed that she only had one more thing on her to-do-before-I-die list—get Maya married. To that effect she placed an ad in the matrimonial classified of the leading newspaper of the city.

Mrs. Chopra gave Maya a look that was one part kindness and three parts pity. While Maya had no disfiguring facial feature like buckteeth or a bulbous nose, she could hardly be called pretty. She had the charm and innocence of youth but could not hope to attract any man based on her looks alone.

"Now, now Maya. Homely is not that bad. See, so many other girls are homely as well," she said pointing to the newspaper. "The real problem is your shyness. Nobody wants to marry a wallflower these days. I wish you had more personality. Like me," Mrs. Chopra mused loudly. "Why, even Mrs. Mathur, from 7B was telling me that she could never imagine any daughter of mine could be so dispirited. I don't know what will happen to you." Mrs. Chopra shook her head in the most melancholy manner.

Maya shrank beside her mother. It was true she thought. She had no identity of her own. She was Mrs. Chopra's daughter to everybody around her. Even at the dance school, most of the students did not know her name. They just called her "*didi*" or "*aunty*." Maya felt like a speck of dust, tumbling through the crowded streets, swerving to avoid the cars and buses and rickshaws, and retiring at the end of the day into one of the thousands of tiny apartments that lit up the night sky as numerous as the stars in the Milky Way and much more anonymous. "Who would want to marry me without looks or personality or any talent?" she wondered as she got into bed later that night. She hugged the bed sheets and looked around the room where she had grown up. She hated the thought of leaving, but the thought of being a spinster was even more terrifying. She crept under the covers to muffle her sobs.

According to Mrs. Chopra, the only way to secure a good husband was through a good dowry. Mrs. Chopra worried incessantly about the peculiar Indian custom of dowry. Though dowry was banned—a criminal offense—and civil people, the kind she wanted as in-laws for Maya, would never ask for dowry, it was customary for the bride's parents to present the bride and groom with expensive gifts—a car, a house, furniture or at the very least a motorcycle. But even without these gifts, weddings were expensive events, and Mr. Chopra had left behind only a small life insurance policy and an even smaller pension.

Mr. Chopra had no family surviving him that Mrs. Chopra could appeal to. Mrs. Chopra, an only child herself, had few cousins and other distant relatives but nobody she felt comfortable asking for help. Instead she turned to her friends and neighbors who all graciously decided to help her host the wedding in the courtyard of their apartment complex to keep the cost to a minimum.

But the question of dowry remained. The only gift Mrs. Chopra had to offer was apartment 5B. It was a modest nine hundred square feet apartment with two bedrooms, a living cum dining room, a compact kitchen and a small balcony off which one could hang clothes to dry. It faced west and received the full glare of the afternoon sun which made it rather uncomfortable to sit in the living room after 2 p.m. The apartment building was only thirty years old but looked considerably older. The maintenance was not what it should have been, and the walls were in need of paint. But the neighbors were friendly, and it stood a mere two blocks from a busy and well-connected intersection where one could hail a bus to most parts of the city.

To Maya's pleasant surprise, the laws of physics work as well in marriage markets as they do in the depths of an atom. For all the "homely" girls there are an equal and opposite number of "homely" boys looking for life partners. And despite all the concerns of parents, and the contrivance of astrologers and matchmakers, marriages, as the old adage goes, are often made in heaven and everything falls into place.

His name was Manoj. He was a mild mannered postal worker at the district post office. He would have been considered a great catch if not for his meager salary and an unfortunate case of acne in adolescence that had left deep craters on both cheeks and forehead.

Manoj saw Maya only once before the wedding. It had been an unfortunate meeting in many ways. Mrs. Chopra had drawn the curtains in the living room to keep out the harsh afternoon sun. As a result the room had been rather dim (but no cooler for Mrs. Chopra's efforts). Somebody had seated Maya to his left in an attempt to allow for conversation. But Mrs. Chopra had sat directly opposite him, dominating the room and the conversation. It had been an awkward angle to turn and talk to Maya who had kept her head bowed the entire time out of confusion and shyness. Manoj had not been able to get a good look at her.

But despite the unsatisfactory nature of the meeting, Manoj had agreed to the match. It seemed the least offensive of all the other proposals he had received so far. There was also the future inheritance of apartment 5B. But he couldn't shake a nagging doubt made worse only by Mrs. Chopra's determined efforts to keep him from meeting Maya again before the wedding.

Finally, the wedding day arrived. Apartment 5B was festooned with mango leaves strung across the main entrance while colored powders decorated the floor. The groom's wedding party threaded its way through the narrow lanes towards Paradise Apartments. Manoj felt a slow churn in his stomach that had started when he had mounted the horse to make his customary entrance as a groom. As Paradise Apartments drew near, the butterflies blossomed into crows battering their wings against his stomach. He felt a cold fear grip him. He could not remember Maya's face.

Some body thrust a bottle into his hands. It smelled of cheap country whisky.

"Drink up, for the night ahead," his brother slurred from below.

"I need to talk with you," said Manoj pushing the bottle away. "I . . . I don't know if I can do this."

"That is what we all feel, little brother, hence the need for this," said his brother thrusting the bottle towards Manoj once again.

"Are you happy?" asked Manoj. "Would you get married again if you had to?" Manoj asked his voice straining to rise above the din.

The answer was lost in the cacophony of noise that some called music.

Manoj found himself being seated in a maroon upholstered chair in the courtyard of Paradise Apartments. The chair had a high back and gilded arm rests, much like the thrones of kings and queens in mythological tales. Somebody had strung garlands of marigolds in the back along with some twinkling electric lights. Manoj nervously wiped his sweaty palms as he sat waiting for Maya. Future neighbors lounging on their balconies looked down at him. Some children ran up to where he had been seated and stared at him. When he smiled, they scowled and ran away.

Finally Maya emerged, dressed in a red bridal sari edged with gold. She was flanked on either side by two women who gently guided her towards the covered canopy. Maya's head and face were veiled in the tradition of Hindu weddings and so the first thing Manoj noticed was her feet. She was barefoot and her feet were covered with intricate henna designs. She had on silver anklets and her toes were painted to match her sari. She had dainty feet and Manoj was captivated by each step they took—the rise and fall of the arch of the feet accompanied by silver bells. A rhyme stirred in his memory about bells and toes, but it had been many years since he had been in school. He could not remember the rhyme.

He noticed Maya had the same henna patterns on her hand. He knew from his cousin's wedding the previous summer that it took hours for the henna to be applied and many more for it to dry. The henna when applied was a black, wet paste that slowly baked with the warmth of the body and left behind a deep rust color. According to folklore, the deeper the color of a bride's henna, the greater the love of her husband would be. Maya's henna was very dark. Her mother must have been pleased—a good omen.

Somebody prodded him and brought him out of his musings. By now Maya was right in front of him. She stood head bowed, garland in hand, ready to commit to a life together. Her face was still partially hidden by the veil. Only her chin and the lower thrust of her lip, outlined in red, was visible. The priest was chanting in Sanskrit and indicating that the bride and groom should garland each other. He saw Maya's lips tremble. This was the moment of finality. He felt a spasm of panic. What if Maya had not got a good look at him either that day? What if she saw his acne ravaged face now and refuse to garland him?

Slowly Maya raised her head. They looked at each other for a moment, and Maya smiled. Manoj's fears vanished. He had never seen a woman so radiant and alive. The warmth of Maya's henna reflected in her eyes. Maya stood before him, in all her bridal finery, proud, happy, content. Manoj wondered how he could have been so blind to her beauty before. He told her that night that she was the most beautiful woman alive.

"You've been watching too many movies," she told him. "Or maybe you need to wear glasses."

He shook his head. He could not explain it, but Maya seemed transformed. She was no longer the shy girl he had met briefly that hot, uncomfortable afternoon but was now a mature confident woman.

In a few days they moved into apartment 5B. Maya took down the now brown and shriveled up mango leaves that still hung across the door and swept up the remnants of the colored powder used to decorate the floor. Manoj took down the Chopra nameplate and placed an order for a new one. Life returned to normal for the residents of Paradise Apartments with the exception of Mrs. Chopra who cried bitterly all the way to the railway station. She had been persuaded by Maya to take a long vacation and visit all the pilgrimage sites she had ever wanted to see before returning home.

Karen Kozicki ~ *Silhouettes in Time*

Patricia Seitz ~ *Snowplay*

Linda Bigness ~ *The Edge of Heart*

Barbara Nevaldine ~ *Hats*

Off-Track Bet

It's a bad bet
said the man who's spent a lifetime
handicapping horses, selecting
daily doubles, quinellas and boxed exactas,
losing thousands and winning hundreds.

But now we're talking about life.
What three docs said isn't good:
biopsy, CT scan, tumors,
no surgery but chemotherapy
with its misery of nausea
and loss of lovely silver hair.
We already know what quality
of living comes vomitous and bald.

The fourth doc thinks out loud,
sizes up the field, handicaps
on the backside of Cancer Center note pad,
inks out a plan, and looks up:
Fifty-fifty.

I brighten; he sits,
still glum, thin, grey, dull.
Fifteen? That's a long shot.

No, no, I amplify, clarify
as I often must in this partnership
of love: *Fifty, not fifteen.*
Fifty, that's like the bets I place,
the ones that always pay something.

Fifty-fifty?
He looks up, more animated
than he's been in weeks.
That's a good bet.

The Dancer

Jackie Bartley

After the accident, he couldn't walk anymore,
but if there were music playing, he could dance.
The mind swings open and shut like a door.

He'd waltz or tap or swing to any score
alone or with a partner. It made no sense:
after the accident, he couldn't walk anymore.

But memory, like the fish that takes the lure,
loves the wiggle and shimmer of resonance.
The mind swings open and shut like a door,

an electric eye sensing its own shadow;
when daylight hits a certain way it doesn't
stay closed. He couldn't walk anymore,

but when music lapped the shores,
some muscle memory wakened at the glance
and his mind swung open and shut like a door.

The body is greater than the sum
of its parts. After the accident, he could dance
though he couldn't walk anymore.
The mind swings open and shuts like a door.

I imagine the poison

—in memory of Margaret Launius

Jennifer Heatley

While you were sleeping on the way to chemo
that beautiful Friday morning
from the serene and loving quiet circling around us, I realized
that the thirty-nine-mile drive was only roughly 1/2500th
the length of the bloodways
of the body.

If they were to be unwoven and laid out,
they would circle around
this spinning gem of a planet
four times.

(And so would I walk
around this world
for a cure.)

I thought about the life blood of you
and while I sat beside you, with the new poison pumping
I tried with all my might to imagine that the poison was sunlight
shining through your veins with a warmth that heals
to the bone.

I imagined the poison was fresh, robust air
entering you through the medi-port window in your chest
blowing the cancer cells adrift as if they were simply dust
that had gathered on drapes.

I imagined the poison was like chicken broth, soup for the soul
glistening and golden with the sweet fatty innards of love,
floating full of the tender care of mothers, grandmothers,
daughters, sisters, and ancestors who believed
there was nothing that chicken stock
could not cure.

And I imagined the poison was like the water in Dorothy's bucket
and that the cancer cells would shrink and melt
like the Wicked Witch
of the West.

And I imagined the poison was a long line-up of protestors marching,
holding flags that said "Peace Now!" and "Make Love,
Not War."

In the line-up were veterans who donned welding masks
and melted their machine guns into a giant peace sign.

I protest this cancer.
And I chant to myself:
May peace be in this body.

Send in the sunlight.
Air. Water.
Chicken stock.
Protestors.
And peace.

I said a silent prayer while we were waiting for the oncologist.
I imagined that the poison was seed and soil.

(May life and landscape
begin sprouting up again.)

May these nesting grounds fill up with birds
fledging from the watershed
of spirit and hope.

May they rise up
through the branches of your body
and call out
with their song
of Life.

Negative

Karen Holmberg

It was the dead of winter, and the headlines
        in my blood read the odds of Downs
                had collapsed to 1 in 20. I set
the alarm to see the predawn
            meteor shower, a veil of debris
                        we pass through every year,
                        our atmosphere's abrasive sac
                        igniting a star's
death matter. Fresh snow over the boot-tops, a day-
old crescent moon,
                Orion's belt
            a pinch of stones dropped
            and scattered, zirconia bright. In his sword
            a nebula, a blur of star nursery.

A spark glowed into being
        and slid across the sky,
                deliberate, needle-bright.

                              In my sonogram,
the tech had moved the pointer to
        a luminous round of calcium
        in the heart, to conjoined-twin
        cysts of water in
the fetal brain. *Soft markers,*
                he called them.

                Attached to you, to the idea
of you, dread regressed me:
        I watched the jittery cold glitter
            of the stars, a cloud of comet dust
            so wide dispersed the flashes come
            just once per minute near
                      the Great Bear's tail, and thought
            of the dusty orbits of

riding lessons, posting the trot what seemed
like wordless hours. My knees gripping
the piston-work.
                                    So much
                expected of me, tethered
to the champion's gaze.
I couldn't pull my eyes
        from the shining slopes
        of the shoulder, the harp of the ear
        turning round to my click,
the blade of the neck
                brindled dark with sweat.

It was a relief to be rained out, to spend
        my five dollar bill at the rock and mineral shop, digging
                geodes from the wooden crate to weigh
                        in my hand's
        scale, the lighter
the more desirable. I'd browse baskets
of peacock ore, flashier than fuel-film
on water, unworkable chips of opal
        vialed in mineral oil and giving tiny spits
                of orange or green-blue iridescence;
                        tangerine calcites, Dalmation
                        jasper, Herkimer diamonds like
                        faceted vinegar, moss agate
whose wintry pools of waterweed I'd crouch
                before, while the owner's diamond blade
                        droned through the head I chose.

Entered, it gave
        a little vulcan sigh. Halved, its gut might glow
the neon green and magenta
                of reef fish under black light, crystals
                        fine and wetly grained as a tongue.

                        Now I had become an opened world:
                a bruise marked the large-gauge
needle's passage through my varied levels
        of resistance until, almost audibly, it breached
                the fibrous womb. On ultrasound, a vortex
        reached a finger through the cloudy ceiling
                        toward a hummock
                        of rump and shoulders, then all went opaque,
                        the core of cyclone in a wave breaking

thunderless in me.

The doctor tugged
the balky plunger till it filled
with cloudy gold, a corpuscular ore
to be sluiced and pulped, winnowed in the centrifuge
so that the *x*'s squat-linked or languid,
draping like bows, could be untangled
and aligned in pairs
and photographed.

Wedges
of petrified wood, slices of agate dyed
gentian violet.
When I can't
sleep I still wander those aisles, reach
into crates for blocks swaddled
in limp newsprint,

rock candy amethyst
from Brazil, snowflake
obsidian's stilled blizzard.
Magnetite to dredge
through roadside sand till it furs itself in filings,
in a mole's velvet. The world all ore, all poles.

Is *I* still

so precarious, so trembling:
a compass needle teetering on a frictionless pin?

As *you*
were precarious:
building in me, perhaps
with some simple math awry
in the blueprints.

Your cranium of cave lakes. The comet in your heart,
its flaring coma.

At an antique mall
I'd found glass negatives wrapped in packs of four or five
in butcher paper. On the backs
the emulsion of gelatin and silver salts
puckered and curled
from the corners, a blistered skin.
With copper tape and solder I fused

their edges, the quicksilver chasing
the flux which vaporized to puffs
of sweet acidic smoke.
Though the seams were clotted, my hurricanes
were stable. Candle-kindled,
a beekeeper offered up
the void of hive, while cloudlet
galaxies hovered in a collect of time
around his head.

Girls with sweet
enigma mouths, with
eye-windows for flame.   I could see them
from the yard
for I set them in the window, let them burn
into the night.

I was afraid
to put you out,
my votives   *I beg of you*
my latest altars   *Let it be negative—*

and it was
lucid as the charge
on an ion, a magnet's pole,
my blood's *O negative*
when the doctor called and let you live.

Well Child Visit March 2008

Kelley Jean White

The four year old's crying, the baby's hitting
me—they both need to get caught up on shots—
their mother's on the phone, she doesn't care
about anything I say, half asleep
now she's mumbling something about babies'
fathers, and what she'll do when they get home
        tonight. The little girls want to go home.
        They don't want to be here. The mother hits
        the older girl on the arm, the baby's
        getting quiet now, big-eyed, the upshot
        of her sister's screams, she pretends to sleep—
        I have to say something. I have to care.
But how can I say "That's no way to care
for children?" when this isn't my place. Home
for me is a safe little town. I sleep
in a safe house in a safe room. I hit
some lucky number, good school, my babies'
healthy, their father's rich, we hear gunshots
        but they aren't aimed at us. These kids get shot
        at routinely. And their mother does care.
        But what can she do. She had two babies
        before she was fifteen. Now she's homeless—
        home's the boyfriend's mother's porch—they all sleep
        rolled up in their coats. When she talks she hits
herself on the head. Some kind of tic, hit
hit. She asks me if I heard about the shots
at their day care on the news. They were sleeping
on their cots at Precious Angels Day Care
and bullets came through the walls of the home
next door. I gasp. Your kids? You? Your babies?
        Yes. But no one got hurt. Not one baby.
        A couple of windows got knocked out, hit
        in the crossfire of gang fighting. Home
        boys. Outside, one of the fathers got shot

but he's gonna make it. He'll be sleeping
a long time though, he's in intensive care.
It's seven. I want to go home and sleep.
Can't care. Can't let this reality hit me.
I smile. I tell her baby shots save lives.

Lois Dorschel ~ *Vole Village*

Mrs. Doctor Powell

W. Soyini Powell

She knew that I had saved her life. Last night she lay in the ER room number eleven with 18-week twins, both dead, lying on the stretcher between her legs. Pain racked her 19-year-old body, her face contorted with each spasm of her uterus as it tried to empty itself. The pungent, slightly sweet but definitely malodorous aroma assaulted my nose as I approached her room. A thought popped into my head from my Harlem Hospital residency days; a seasoned nurse said in her lilting Jamaican accent, "I can tell she water broke, my nose knows the smell of liquor." I knew that normal amniotic fluid has a distinctive smell like fermenting apricot brandy. My nose knew my patient-to-be was infected; her pregnancy overwhelmingly contaminated with bacteria whose metabolic by-products settled over the entire room like a toxic nuclear cloud.

Chorioamnionitis kills, causing premature labor, eventually sepsis and finally maternal death.

Like the captain of a ship, I took over and organized the chaos that played out before me into a treatment plan. Hard-wired into my brain, my words and actions poured forth, calming and guiding the ER staff and doctors: GYN was here.

I introduced myself to my patient, "Hi, my name is Dr. Powell, I'm going to take care of you"—simple, direct, and to the point.

The next morning I do my hospital rounds checking up on any patients t"hat have been admitted on the gyn service. My young patient is sitting up in bed, intravenous fluids pouring life saving antibiotics into her left antecubital vein. She is grateful, wants to express her appreciation and to introduce the doctor who made the pain and bleeding go away.

"Mom, this is Mrs. Powell. She took care of me last night." She is soft spoken, eyes alert in spite of the 7 a.m. early morning hour.

"No, Dear, I'm Doctor Powell" was my quick, automatic response as I took my hand out of my white lab coat pocket, right index finger sweeping upward to point directly to my name tag. My hospital ID was clipped to the upper breast pocket, my name embroidered across in burgundy ink.

"Oh, sorry. Mom, this is Mrs. Doctor Powell," she said to her mother who sat quietly in a small metal chair near her hospital bed.

I am the only African American female OBGYN working in this predominantly African American impoverished community. It's my Calling! I've come to realize this after years of working in academic medicine. One cold winter morning I sat listening to a Unitarian minister's sermon in my church, participating in the Sunday morning's "most segregated hour" despite Unitarian Universalist's liberal ideologies; I sat within a sea of white faces listening to the passionate words of a white minister. He was discussing being *Called* to ministry.

"Just what is a Calling?" he queried. "A Calling is when you find what you love to do and then find a need for it out in the larger world."

I was moved; a warm tide of emotion washed over me like a wave in a not so calm, blue Caribbean Sea jolting me awake, alert, focused. Yes, I had an epiphany! My work in this West Philadelphia neighborhood with the working poor, underserved, undereducated and predominantly African American women—this was my Calling. All of my life experiences, my trials and struggles through the predominantly white male culture of medical education and practice in this country, all of the pressures in academic medicine to "publish or perish," all of the hours spent away from my family, my two small children (who after my forty-eight hours absence on call would dance around me on their little legs singing, "Mommy's home, Mommy's home") had led me here. This was my place, this community that appreciated my presence, that loved the fact that not only was I a woman, but that I looked like them: brown skinned with golden brown sister-locks usually swept up off my neck and wrapped in a colorful scarf; dangly, funky ear rings adorning my earlobes. Yes, I'd found *my Calling*. I was saving lives, educating women on the importance of primary prevention and early detection, you know, Well Medicine not Sick Medicine.

This 19-year-old who had just lost her babies, who narrowly missed forfeiting her own life, with her mother/grandmother-not-to-be sitting by her bedside, saw me as one with her. In our culture Mrs. confers respect. It is a title children are taught to use to show respect for their elders and for people with authority. Mrs. Ruth, never just Ruth. So even though I know that twelve years and more of vigorous, dedicated education and training to obtain my MD title surely must trump the Mrs. title, my grateful young patient wrapped me in our culture giving me what in her mind was the ultimate title of respect; she put that Mrs. right out front, first above all of the rest and called me Mrs. Doctor Powell. And for that moment, I just let it be.

Inheritance

—For A.C.H.

Joyce Holmes McAllister

Your eyes search the room
before you split the silence
with your voice.
"Where will you put
the antique chest
my mother left to me?"

I hear the words and
know your thought,
soundless as the plaster,
paint, wood, reflected in
your eye. I fashion
a reply—casual, steady
as your tone. "Why,
there against the
window wall."
You smile, "That will
be good," you say.

We talk of antique chests
instead of shortened time,
avoid each other's eyes,
turn our heads away;
and hope that death,
confused and spent as we,
may also lose the way.

Stranded

M. Frost

I last saw the cow standing on a red roof,
her gold coat thick with mud, her eyes dark
and calm. Sunlight browned deep water
as it rose from the river to flood her barn.

I looked back across an outboard motor
as the creeping water buried her hooves.
I pondered how cows swim, their opposing legs
plunging like pistons, their heads bobbing for air.

I remembered a heifer calf stranded by the tide
outside Tralee after sunset. She followed her dam
faithfully into the brackish water of the bay,
her legs dipping into the rising sea salt and reeds,
her little snout silver and high as she swam.

I should do so well outside my element.
I should hold up my head and loosen my legs,
swallow salt and mud to sustain me; rise, brown
and dripping, into the light of a farther shore.

A Breath

V. P. Loggins

Sometimes the dead
go on living. Like
the sound mourning
doves make when

they take flight. I've
come upon them
in the shade, among
the ferns, where green

lies too deep for names,
and they have flown
fearsomely alive with
their wings whistling

out of the dark. No
windhover, sun-washed
and buoyed, circling on
an updraft of joy, but

a quickened necessity
to fly from one green
shade to another. This
too is a kind of death,

an act of loneliness,
remaining, once heard,
like the last breath cupping
before the flight has come.

BREAKING NEWS

Stephanie Elliott

Yes, no, yes, no, yes. I wish they'd make up their dumb old minds. The Yes/No Game, I call it. Seems like a game no one can win. Mommy and Daddy play it all the time lately. And I never get to play. I don't care so much. I'm just fine being me in my bedroom every day. And I'm trying hard to watch TV. Clifford the Big Red Dog, my favorite, is on now. I just turn up the sound, that's all. Then I can't hear them, almost. I know how to play my own games.

Funny Clifford stands as high as a house, he's that big! He never hurts anyone, though. He's so big you can ride him because Clifford's giant, and he can take you anywhere faster than a car or a plane. But it's hard to find a doghouse for him. It's cool because Clifford gets giant-size everything because he's special. That's what happens when you're special. You get cool stuff, and it's not like everyone else's stuff. Clifford is too big and too red to be growing up with regular people. You can only see him on TV. That's a kind of real, too.

Because if he were really real, regular people would probably not know how to feed and walk him. Some people would be afraid of him because he's so red and bigger than everyone else. But he's always ready to help out. And so, some people want to be nice to him. And then he licks them. The people who have him as their pet on TV know how to feed and walk him, and they're not so afraid at all. So, his people are happy, too! Seems like it always works out happy for Clifford. Me being real, I don't want to be as different as Clifford.

But I don't care that he's so different.

My dog Mike is really real. His whole name's Michelangelo, after my brother's favorite Teenage Mutant Ninja Turtle, who died—my brother Denny died, not the Ninja Turtle and not Mike. Mike did get sick once but he lived longer than Denny. Anyway . . . I'll probably never live as long as Mike, or even be as happy as Clifford—Oh great, now they're showing BREAKING NEWS over my cartoons.

Wow! A twister! Don't look like anything's breaking, though. That swirling air cone is big like Clifford, spinning over all the houses, bigger even than Clifford. Like to plop a big blob of Claire's cold Vanilla Fudge Smash ice-cream on that winding air cone, if you could get it to stop a minute. Then, I'd eat it—I'm hungry. Damn! (shouldn't say that) WHERE is my breakfast?

Anyway . . . everyone on TV is so shiny and pretty. Those twisters, I saw a girl

40 ◆ *The Healing Muse 11*

once with her mommy on TV and they lived after it spun on them and their house fell. The mommy was hugging and kissing the daughter. Some neighbors didn't live. But the people on TV said nice things about them, how they were good and nice neighbors. They all got on TV and they were getting new stuff and better new homes. Even though they cried. And a lot of times the people they say are dead are still alive on TV. Denny was never on TV, though.

But I think he's in heaven.

I was thinking about that and wondering if earthworms go to heaven. Because one time, while I sat in front of the porch with Grandma sitting up there watching (she told me before that I shouldn't pick out the earthworms from the ground, that we needed them, and that earthworms were part of helping us all live and that I should leave them there to do in the ground what Mother Nature said they were supposed to be doing and not to even dare think of killing them. But a boy from down the street told me that if you cut an earthworm in half that it'll grow a head on the back half and then be two alive earthworms) and so I snuck in front of Grandma an earthworm out of the muddy ground and I took my digging shovel and made it in two. I thought Grandma would be happy if I made two earthworms out of one and that we would be better off because now we had two earthworms to help us live.

But ya know what? That bad old earthworm did wriggle on both pieces for awhile at first and then didn't anymore. I don't think Grandma saw, so I figured everything'd be okay, it being up there in heaven and all. . . . And I wonder . . . if I go to heaven, maybe me and Denny can be like the two dead halves of the earthworm put back together and come alive again. Mommy would like that I think. . . . So . . . I can't go out even past the porch much anymore because I got this dumb old sickness. Hardly no one gets it, accept Denny, my dead brother. And me. I'd try to say its name but every time I try, well, my tongue and lips don't work to say it. Mommy says No, I shouldn't get the operation and that it won't make me better, and Daddy says Yes, I should get the stupid operation and that it will make me better.

Anyway . . . I can't go much of anywhere now that I got the hard-to-say sickness, after I went to the doctor and he all sticking me with them hurting needles and making me do stuff like walk and cough and jabbing my belly, and he said so that I got it, so my friends don't play any more—Oooh, now the BREAKING NEWS says the twister is at Laurelton, the town over where we sometimes get to go on Sundays if I eat all my burger, and it's sure spinning. Looks like if I were out there—which I'm not—that wind'd fly my hat right off, leaving me bald as an eagle. That's why I wear them, the hats, so as no one sees that I'm bald.

Oh, finally. Finally, Mommy's making my breakfast. I can smell the toast smelling so good, it's smelling the whole house up like warm toast. I can hear her and Daddy and yelling loud, too, and the good toast smell isn't so good anymore because now I smell burnt smell. And it's clouds of smoke in here. And now

Mommy's yelling and popping the toast and she's opening the squeaky garbage lid. Slam! And now everything's quiet. But the burnt burns my eyes bad.

So I was saying . . . Laurelton's where we get to play miniature golf. I like it lots, but we don't go much since Mommy and Daddy been Yesing and Noing over the sickness. But sometimes Daddy'll whisper all secret-like in my ear after burgers, Marylou, let's whip on over to miniature golf. I love when he says that, like a horse's tail whipping off flies (not like Clifford's banging tail, but light and flicking like). So real quick we whip on over to Laurelton and play, and sometimes we whip on back so fast that Mommy doesn't even know we were gone, unless I spill ice-cream on my shirt. That she can see's not from home but come from Claire's Candy Cane where Claire gives me a free Vanilla Fudge Smash ice-cream because she knows I got sick. Mommy would be for sure mad if she knew I'd been out of my room—Oh, where is Clifford? That stupid old twister twirling around BREAKING NEWS on top of Clifford. I'm so hungry. . . . Oh, will ya listen to them. . . . Maybe Daddy's right, I should get cut in half and fixed.

But that earthworm stopped wriggling. . . .

But I can't say for sure. I can't say. Who knows?

I think maybe, maybe I should go tell Mommy and Daddy the BREAKING NEWS that the twister is coming this way, because the miniature golf course for sure looks all broke up now along with Claire's Candy Cane. I'll go tell them. I'll look out my door and see.

Gee, Mommy looks like she wants to lie on the bed, her arms hanging and swinging down. Mommy usually likes to dress white and pretty, Prim and Proper, she always says, but lately she's not at all Prim and Proper. Lately, she wears the same old raggedy big shirt, one of Daddy's old ones, and sometimes she sleeps in it and wakes up and wears it all day and goes asleep again in it.

I feel tired, too. Maybe we need to all go asleep—Oh God, oh God, they're yelling again and I can't tell them nothing about the twister. I'll just go back in my room and change the channel—Where is it, that breakfast I should've had by now? I'm going to say it, Mommy said not to, that it's a bad word. But in my head I can say anything—DAMN!

Damn it, damn, damn, damn them, and damn the operation, and the damn, damn sickness. All go away. Damn them. And where's my breakfast, damn you, damn Mommy! I saw Denny under all them noisy machines. I see at the hospital how they try to make it fun with stupid toys. And stupid stuffed Barney. There's no Clifford there, just damn Barney. They should know I like Clifford best if they're going to operate on me. They should know me.

And I don't want all that special stuff neither, it's not cool special stuff, it's scary special, even Claire's free ice-cream—And smiley fake nurses. That lady nurse is fake, and Dr. Logan, and that man nurse who's with Barney all the time. They don't know me but pretend like best friends, and they don't come to secret miniature golf on Sundays with Daddy and me. They're fake. I know that—And now the twister is at Carney. That's the next town to us where we sometimes walk Mike, but Mommy and Daddy, I can't say shut up or tell them look or listen. And I could die without the operation Daddy says. So I wonder when Daddy says Yes to have the operation does he think that if I get cut in half like the earthworm that I'll still be alive?

But I was wrong about that earthworm.

Maybe Mommy's wrong about saying No.

Damn, you'd think it would be easy to figure out if a person'd be better off or not with an operation, and that it would for sure make us all happy.

Boy, that twister's whipping stuff around like flies off a horse. Even Clifford's house wouldn't be standing. And outside is getting so dark and rainy.

And right there on TV they're saying about us. That's our town's name. Newtown.

I DON'T CARE.

I don't care if the whole damn town of us dies.

And the BREAKING NEWS is saying we better get out.

If that twister broke our house we could hug and kiss and Mommy could be on TV all Prim and Proper again—

SHUT UP.

We better get out.

Please, please, shhh. . . .

   If I shut my door, I can not listen.

And if I shut my TV, there won't be BREAKING NEWS.

And if I go asleep and not tell . . . no one will know . . .

Coma Rise

Tish Pearlman

The white of the room
draped in shimmering light
loses
horizon
If only I could move
I would reach for cool shade
I would follow the shoreline
to the end of spring
I would will my mind to
awaken in starless, motionless
space
where the moon comes and
evaporates like the speed of wings
no longer there

Disembodied

Tish Pearlman

When I die abruptly
I will understand where
the blood has gone:
the blood of wars,
of car accidents,
of petty misunderstandings,
of strange changes in
pressure.
And bones thrown into
shallow graves will speak.
When I die abruptly
I will see smoke rise
I will be the wing transforming
the wind
I will be
cloudless over a
a lapping wave,
and shells uncovered by time
will erase the pattern of
I was here once.
My name is.

A phone call after midnight

Nina Bennett

never brings good news. My father's
bedside dialysis line has clotted again,
third night in a row, after his family
stumbled home from the hospital
to shed tears hidden not only from him,
but from each other.

The doctor says my father, intubated
and less responsive each day,
communicates in the only language
he can access, declares his wishes
to those who will listen.

I drink coffee until daybreak, drive
to my childhood home. Mum
sits on the patio, stares
at the overgrown clematis Dad planted,
shakes her head when I start
to speak. She puts on gardening gloves,
picks up the pruner, clips
until violet flowers spring free,
released from the confines
of tangled vine. Chooses a blossom
the shade of midnight for Dad,

a jolt of color against the white sheets
and metal of the ICU.
Dad died that evening,
his final exhale so gentle
it didn't ruffle the faded
flower resting on his chest.

On the Occasion of the War Finding its Way into My Living Room

Gail Hosking

Funny, how the Vietnam War—or the American War, as the Vietnamese refer to it—returns so quickly as if it never ended when the voice on the phone mentions my father, "the Snake." *It will do my soul good to talk to you about him,* says the stranger after finding me on the Internet by surprise. I sit back on the couch with my feet up and my notebook in hand as I've done many times with similar calls for decades. I write down the details like a reporter getting the facts. I include things like place, time, characters, and dialogue as if I'm writing a novel. They all speak about the good soldier, how the nation owes my father a debt. They all seem surprised to find out my father had children.

I have to admit there is a pride that rises up as I sit there alone with my pen in hand. Odd that after all this time this ex-soldier's casual talk about grease guns and Browning automatics and patrols and C teams and enemy lines and R&R feels like the talk of my childhood. I remember the sounds like a language I learned long ago, buried, and then miraculously speak again. His voice makes this language sound so easy, so every-dayish that it might make a good movie or story. Only this is my life; and everything in my world changed with those words, that war, those men.

This is my father, the protagonist of his story, the soldier who shot up that bar in Saigon when the white mice pulled a weapon on him for nothing. *Like some scene out of the west,* the stranger says, and we both laugh, now forty-five years after the event. The Captain, a father of three, gave him an Article 15, he tells me, some non-judicial punishment, instead of a court martial, fined him two hundred dollars and let him keep his sergeant stripes. "Guy We," my father called him, which meant captain in the Vietnamese he spoke. "Guy We," he said when the police returned him in a chopper back to his jungle base, "I fucked up. I screwed up bad! They're going to bust me."

The Captain says over the phone now, *Snake was the best soldier ever. The most dedicated and courageous man I ever met. I needed him. So we had to work around the system.* The system, he tells me, meant a call from the Colonel who had some other Colonel over his shoulder wanting to "punish the bastard," but the two other men couldn't. *I ask myself again and again,* he repeats with a voice that contains remnants of his Boston years, *was I just another link in the chain of his death? If I had let them kick him out of the army, I knew he'd be a broken man, but this decision I made back in 1965 let him return to Vietnam, let him get that Medal of Honor, let him get killed.*

As the one to soothe him, I say something about my father's need to go out that way, but of course, the thought of his black body bag comforts neither of us. We're left with this story in our laps as the winter snow blows outside my apartment on the eighth floor of an old building, and he keeps turning his head to cough somewhere in Georgia. When we finally get off the phone hours later, I rise only to find my legs like Jell-o, my heart looking for its hinges. Those years crawl inside me to the forefront, and I am alone again holding these memories in my hand like a live grenade.

What comes home from war is there in my living room again, breathing its forsaken men and national shame across the floor. I walk over to the window and linger a while catching a view of snowflakes in the streetlamps below. Very few people are out walking at this cold hour. For a moment, the world out there seems to exist in a separate universe, one that speaks nothing of this anymore. Now, my insides bounce to the rhythm of voice turned back into silence. I cannot settle myself, even as I turn to the stove to make a late dinner.

"Vietnam is passé," a poetry editor recently said to me. "Why do you keep writing about it?"

The Living

Basilia Nwankwo
Dearing Writing Award, Poetry
Student Division

I would steal
short glances at the eyes
of my dying father—reddened, bulging
pronouncing exhaustion, revealing years
of mischievous sons and rebellious
daughters. In the end, I couldn't remember
the years before, when he was well,

Except for one evening—the living
room, walking towards each other, the sunset
warming the tiles, spilling in from the foyer; the anticipation
of his approaching figure like that
of an unfamiliar acquaintance, the air
of a reluctant meeting, and as we each passed
the other, my eyes shot nervously into the dark
folds of a nearby sofa—I felt his eyes upon my back.

I had checked his tubes countless times, and drew
in the scent of his room, like the forceful
inhalation of a rancid stench or toxic marker
as if trying to believe its existence, its realness.
On that night, he stopped me, "Why did you turn away?
Why couldn't you look at me?"
As I fumbled for answers (even now)
and as he lay in the hospital bed, unconscious,
wide-eyed, yet blind to the world,
I couldn't take my eyes off him.

Unease Creeps In

Laurie Oot Leonard

Unease creeps in. An unwelcome visitor in a time of scarcity, who sucks up the cool air, snacks on dried crumbs of possibility, sipping sweet juice of hopefulness, leaving me hungry for the mundane. A 12:15 bride at a noon wedding. A loose cough in 1910. The tired, grim, sweat soaked surgeon. Hipbone cracking on a hard dirt road. The instant before a sharply inhaled breath, the long groan "ummmm," the whimper and the piercing cry of the fallen . . . stillness. A silent void. Then, staccato tapping, mouse scratches, an insistent whisper. "Let me in."

I'd rather sit at a table with boredom as company. Not commenting on peeling damask wallpaper or chintz curtains billowing through an unfixed window. Sip stale Earl Grey from a cracked china cup, swirling sodden leaves, clockwise, hoping to read good fortune. "Nice weather for April," I suggest, a dumb smile lining my dry face. I'd ask after unattractive, grown, far away children and the recipe for bland peach preserves spread on Melba toast, smoothing the red checked, wrinkled cloth beneath my age-spotted hands.

From under, I pull dusty Heinz ketchup boxes, cardboard tearing through my slipping grasp, dumping handfuls of Kodak Instamatic, Polaroid and the few orphan digital prints onto the crimson and white rumpled surface. Moving in day, new buff colored kittens, tenderly placed daffodils and my opened soul. Tens and tens of you and me . . . smiling, close. I deal out each frozen second, separating piles of the decade's span. "You'll take this one. I'll have that."

Snow

Katharyn Howd Machan

falls outside my safe brown home
and I am weeping, I am crying:
this house holds two black-striped cats
but God is a distant palace of whim

allowing my daughter to long for a drug
that turns her into thin gray smoke,
vague lips that lie for survival.
Crystals? They're blowing now

swift and silver and silent as hope
only a mother can ask to find
when the body she's birthed and loves
finds heroin is more important

than giving to the wider world
calling out her name. Snow
beautiful and bright and pure
pours down from a streetlit night

here where I dare write a poem
praying that the girl I bore
is able to look out through a window
and wonder at winter sky.

Sandwich Board

Jennifer Campbell

No turning back
once you pass the first test.
You aren't just you anymore.
The job: march around
fostering need in others.
With limbs restricted,
you bump into door frames
thanks to your newfound
triangular girth, never manage
to put your feet up
long enough to relieve
the pressure of the message.
People always want to rub
your belly, but there's an odd
abandon in your recent enormity.
Your placid wobbling
starts to feel natural
and the luxurious leggy stride
of youth becomes memory—
unwanted, inconceivable,
since all that matters now
is these steps, this largesse,
your secret within.

Who Lets You Go

—*In memory of P.G.*

J.P. Maney

Forget what you've read in books, or
watched in movies, where no one dies
in the aloneness of agony, having arrived

at the correct address, unable to enter.
You may want it; you may be ready.
But your body has no such desire.

In the end, this narrow, hospital night
may be your dungeon:
no mattress, no blanket—the door opened

only after a long wait,
not by love, not by Jesus, but by life's old enemy,
now your best friend—

the one who lets you go.

Silence Over Coffee

Angela M. Giles Patel

If instead,
I told you I had a cancer
would you still sit,
biding your time,
waiting for me to heal?
Would life carry on
in your view of us
as each day my body
was divided, conquered,
one weakened cell after another?

If instead,
I could show you spots
or unnatural shadows
on an X-ray film and say
    here and here and here
    that is where it is,
    that is where I am slowly dying,
would you still simply
pat me on the head
and say "Now, now"?

But I can't
fix my trembling finger
on a single point to tell you
    this is where it hurts
and it's not my fault
I've no black and white image
to prove
I'm being devoured slowly,
painfully being consumed
by my dis-ease.

And while what you say
may be true,

that "this too shall pass,"
any remission just means dormancy.
I must tell you
the fiercest storms
gather strength while resting
and nature's cycles
prey on weakness,
they are meant to destroy first
and then, perhaps, rebuild.

For now we both sit
quietly sipping our morning coffee
you burdened
by my malaise
my dis-order,
me alone,
waiting, hoping for relief.

Pamela Ferris-Olson ~ *Stand-Off*

A Quote from *Ondine*

Clifford Paul Fetters

As the years count higher the entire everything, all the scenes and dialogue
seem as the straw hut of the little pig so easily huffed and puffed to dust.
But the brick one crumbles too, the wolf is huge.

My body feels so un-jointed as if an arm would go over by the sofa
and a leg by the chair and my head is floating near the ceiling fan.
Look out! Like the Scarecrow after the flying monkey attack:

"Well, that's you all over!" The middle messes of not-tragedy and
not-delight creeping in petty pace spread me apart and the center
of me splits into pieces like a hammered walnut. I'm vacuumed

into a hollowness of spreading hours and days to come. I try to be
a sentence in the present tense, the now, but the thoughts spray
like a garden hose all over the patio. Boy, it's easy to forget good,

the disappointments are like dead elephants you're trying to bury in
the back yard. That chore takes all your focus. What did Jordan's priest
say in the film? "Misery is easy, Syracuse. It's happiness you have to work at."

Esperanza Tielbaard ~ *Energize*

Joan Applebaum ~ *Wishing I Could Remember the Violets*

Keeping the Faith

Susan J. Levy

My spiritual story began with my growing up in a Jewish family. Both my parents were conservative in how they practiced their faith. My father's side of the family was orthodox; they kept a kosher house and went to synagogue weekly. Often my dad would take us out to breakfast before Sunday School, and we'd have bacon and eggs. When visiting my grandfather we would have to lie about what we ate, which felt very uncomfortable. This ambivalent foundation in faith carried over to synagogue. I don't remember having any special feelings of connection or understanding for the rabbi or the readings during the high holidays, since they were mostly recited in Hebrew, which I didn't know. Over the years however, I felt a spiritual connection with the prayers as I read them in English and listened to the melodies of the songs. I always loved the cultural traditions, rituals and the Jewish holiday celebrations. It was a family time—yet there was an incongruent feeling surrounding it. I did believe and have faith that God would watch over me and comfort me in times of need.

A major test of my faith occurred in 1976 when my dad was diagnosed with prostate cancer. My family was in shock, as my dad was just fifty-five-years old and had never been seriously ill; he always went for a regular checkup. Apparently something had been missed, since it had metasticized to the bone. My dad began with traditional medicine and soon after began exploring alternative therapies. As a family we had faith in whatever treatment he was doing, whether traditional or complementary. We believed it was making him better. He lived with this disease for six years, living fully until three weeks before he died. This experience opened my eyes, mind, and heart to other ways of looking at life and health, but more importantly, it brought home the importance of love and support from family and friends.

My father's death was very difficult for me. As close as we all were as a family throughout his illness, we all went our own separate ways to grieve. This was very confusing to me at the time. I couldn't understand why we weren't talking about Dad and sharing our feelings of loss. None of my friends had lost a parent or loved one, so I felt that they had difficulty understanding the pain I was in. What I did in my private psychotherapy practice was let my clients know that I was grieving for my dad and that I didn't have all the answers. The act of sharing allowed many of them to go to a new depth of exploring their own personal losses.

Six months after my dad's death, I was still experiencing a lot of emotional pain and aloneness. Elisabeth Kübler-Ross was coming to Atlanta. I knew she was the death and dying "expert." I arrived early for her presentation and sat in the front row. I felt as if she was speaking to me when she said, "I believe when someone dies, they are met by someone who loved them deeply." I knew my dad was okay, and that he was met and watched over through this transition by his mother. I was so taken by Elisabeth Kübler-Ross that a month later I went to a five-day workshop she was giving on Living with Death and Dying. It was there I decided that this was an area I wanted to specialize in my clinical practice. I learned that life-threatening illness affects us physically, mentally, emotionally and spiritually. I furthered my education in this area by going to training groups with Stephanie Simonton, Bernie Siegel, Jeanne Achterberg and others, where I learned techniques like meditation, visualization and also the power of presence and hope and the importance our attitude plays in our healing. These various tools and ideas helped my patients feel a little more in control of some aspects of their life during times of difficulty, uncertainty, and unknowing.

In 1990 I was asked by a friend to give a talk at Common Ground, a day program for people living with HIV/AIDS. This program was a part of Atlanta Interfaith AIDS Network. I loved the fact that people of different religions were coming together in working for a common cause. I found a spiritual home for myself and felt a strong connection the moment I walked thru the door. I ran weekly support groups at this program along with an AIDS Survival Group and volunteered for almost ten years. The spiritual renewal I got from this work led me to create a sacred space within my home—a meditation room. I created a daily ritual of reading Jewish prayers, meditating or listening to sacred music. During difficult personal times I prayed to feel more connected to God. Two of my colleagues and I started a group in 1995 that lasted for five years entitled, "On Being with Death and Dying." We trained therapists who were interested in working in a contemplative way with people dealing with life threatening illness. As a community we learned to meditate together, bear witness, and share the experience.

My life between 1983 and 2001 contained typical life choices people go through: marriage, divorce, and good physical health. Everything was moving along smoothly in my life. I was feeling secure in the ways my spiritual life was integrating into my professional life. I felt bolstered by a thriving private practice and energized by a new romance, and I was looking forward to moving into a new home. Then in the spring of 2001 on the day of move, I had a personal experience that shook my foundation. I was running errands when I felt a snap inside my head, and then it was as if I were in an odd sort of movie in slow motion. I began experiencing some confusion and disorientation and exhibiting behavior that was truly out of character for me. I wrote a check to the wrong person, even though I'd known the intended recipient for years. I drove to three stores and got angry with the clerks who said they could not accept or change my Brazilian money left over from a recent trip. I went to a bakery and bought several unnecessary pies and

cakes to take to my date's house. I then went home to dress for dinner without re-
alizing I was already late for our rendezvous and left my house unaware that I was
wearing two different styled shoes. My peculiar behavior continued as I drove in
the opposite direction from where I needed to go, and when I got lost, I called my
boyfriend for directions several times. I then spotted a homeless person wearing
dirty clothes, standing on the side of the exit with a sign saying PLEASE HELP I
HAVE AIDS. I rolled down the window, started crying and told him I was lost and
needed help. He offered to give me directions, and in my confusion, I allowed him
to get into my car. He managed to guide me to a police officer, though much later
I discovered he'd stolen my wallet. The police officer spoke with my boyfriend and
waited with me until he arrived with my friends in tow. They immediately drove
me to the emergency room.

Once in the hospital, attendants drew blood, ran a CAT scan, and administered various tests. When hours passed without a diagnosis, my behavior grew
even more erratic. I grew agitated and tore the IVs out of my arm. I didn't know
what was going on, and I was scared. After more than eight hours of tests and no
explanation, one of the doctors suggested I was having a psychotic episode. This
diagnosis foreshadowed the events to come.

The next morning I left the ER with a close friend and my boyfriend. My
friend had arranged an emergency evaluation with a colleague who was a child
psychologist, as my therapist had recently moved to another state. During this ses-
sion, I said things that had no foundation in truth. For reasons I will never fathom,
I watched myself "confess" that I had been molested as a child, even though it
was a complete fabrication. I was unable to stop the words from coming out of
my mouth. After two hours, the child psychologist, who knew nothing about my
stable mental history, suggested I be further evaluated at another hospital.

My friends drove me to Peachford Hospital, an inpatient psychiatric facility. I
still wasn't exhibiting any physical symptoms, only the confusion, disorientation,
and agitation I had been experiencing. The doctor I met with upon my arrival
asked me a series of questions, the last one being, "Are you suicidal?" Thinking I
was being funny, I said, "Yes." This response turned out to be the worst mistake of
my life. At this point, a vortex appeared beneath me and began sucking me down.
I was immediately admitted and forced to undergo a mandatory evaluation. I raged
against the decision, because I knew I was not suicidal. Regardless, the doctor
administered several antipsychotic drugs. For five days I existed in a drugged,
zombie-like state, not believing where I was or why I was there. Even through the
haze of the drugs, I felt a tremendous amount of shame and humiliation. My psychiatric diagnosis now felt more like punishment—rather than help. How could
this be happening to me? What was happening to me? Would this go on forever?
I had always assumed I would one day develop some kind of physical illness like
cancer or diabetes, but never that something would be wrong with my brain. I
was terrified. My friends and family were baffled. My therapist of thirteen years
was finally contacted, and she informed my doctor, "This is not Susan; something

neurological is going on." The psychiatrist didn't pay attention to her.

After leaving Peachford, I lived like a nomad with various friends, since my new home was still unfinished. I attempted to resume work but soon realized I could not focus on my clients. My therapist friends took over my practice, and for two months my confusion and disorientation did not improve. I did things like walk into a closet, not knowing what to do. At this time, these friends suggested to my family that I go to McLeans Hospital in Boston, since it was one of the best facilities in the country. While waiting for a bed to open up in the unit, I stayed in Ohio for the weekend with my brother and his family. I couldn't remember how to take a shower, so my sister-in-law bathed me. I was so scared of what was to come. At McLeans, I was placed in a unit for Dissociative Disorders with seriously disturbed patients. It was straight out of *One Flew Over the Cuckoo's Nest*, including the stark, rundown environment, moldy dark brown food, and highly disturbed patients. During this time of terror I managed to keep a journal. I also kept in contact with family and friends, and prayed often. I would recite the words of the Shema, "*Shema Yisra'el Adonay Eloheynu, Adenay Ehad,*" the holiest of Jewish prayers ("*Hear O Israel, the Lord is our God, The Eternal One alone*"), desperately praying to God to help me. I was mistakenly overmedicated on my first day. I asked to see a neurologist. Eight days later, they finally scheduled my appointment. I sat with the neurologist while she heard my story, looked at my MRI and said to me, "You had a TIA, a Transient Ischemic Attack—a mini stroke affecting the limbic area of your brain. A woman does not have her first psychotic break at fifty-three." Even after the surprise and relief of her words—some form of an answer I had been hoping for—I was still frightened, because my condition was not improving. She then called in the head of the department and discussed my diagnosis. She informed me of several cases of women my age who had also been similarly misdiagnosed. She suggested I stay in town with a friend for two weeks so she could supervise my healing process. She told me it would take approximately three months for my brain to heal. I contacted a friend who lived in the Boston area. He and his family opened their home to me, cared for me, accompanied me to the doctor, and watched over me as if they were my family—just as my close friends in Atlanta had.

Up to this point in my life, my faith in doctors and our medical system had gone unchallenged. Now, however, I couldn't understand or justify all of my misdiagnoses and the lack of communication between doctors. The majority hadn't been willing to accompany me on my journey as I had always done with my clients. I expected they would do this for me. I experienced a series of events with medical professionals where I felt dehumanized, misperceived, and dismissed. I was sent to a neurologist who kept me waiting for three hours and then spent three hours preaching religion and only ten minutes doing any tests. A neuropsychologist thought I might have a form of dementia. A psychiatrist said to me, "We don't know what caused this. We may never know." I interpreted these comments to mean that I might stay this way and never get better. My belief was that I had to understand the cause of what was happening in order to get better.

My personal faith was constantly challenged during this time of crisis. Where was God? Would I ever be okay again? It's been ten years since my TIA, and though I still deal with these questions, my internal landscape feels very different now. I have climbed out of that horrible hole. My relationship survived the crisis and has continued for almost ten years. I have a wonderful family—my mother, two brothers and their families. Three and a half years ago I got my first pet, Lucky, a King Charles Cavalier Spaniel. I enjoy spending time with my dear and supportive friends and continue to travel, practice qigong and Tai Chi, take daily walks, and I have resumed playing the piano and knitting. Most importantly, I have faith. I no longer focus on getting answers. As Miriam Greenspan, author of *Healing Through the Dark Emotions* says, "Befriended fear unexpectedly expands our capacity for joy. And conscious despair can become the doorway to a more resilient faith in life." My experience has taught me that the essence of being on a spiritual journey is being willing to embrace the "not knowing"—some experiences may never be understood. I remind myself daily that if I have the courage to sit quietly with my fears and sadness, I will find my way.

Kathleen Gunton ~ *Looking for Tiny Miracles*

Barriers in Health Care:
Language, Culture, and Education

Zin Min Tun
Dearing Writing Award, Prose
Student Division

One Saturday morning during my medicine clerkship, I got a call from Thida, a Burmese friend, asking me to interpret for a child and his family in the hospital. I met the parents first; they seemed to be confused, distressed, and frustrated. They had just heard the ICU doctor tell them that their twelve-year-old son would die soon.

Phyo was diagnosed with Duchenne muscular dystrophy (DMD). When I met him in the Pediatric Intensive Care Unit (PICU), he was lying in bed and looked exhausted. And yet he remained calm and told his parents that he would be okay. The pediatric ICU doctor and a pediatric cardiologist then took us to a quiet family room. They told the parents that Phyo had heart failure and there was nothing that they could do to cure it. The child's father asked me how Phyo's leg weakness was related to his heart condition. I realized that the parents didn't understand what was happening to Phyo.

Phyo, born in Thailand, developed difficulty in walking and in getting up from the floor when he was two. At the age of seven, Phyo's family came to America as refugees, and he began to receive regular pediatric care. He was later referred to a pediatric neurologist, Dr. Dan, for his bilateral progressive leg weakness. A muscle biopsy confirmed the diagnosis of DMD. Dr. Dan explained these results to the family using a Burmese interpreter, but the parents' limited education and possibly that of the interpreter meant they did not grasp the nature of the disease, how it would progress, or how it would affect Phyo.

DMD is an inherited disorder. Some of the clinical features of DMD include pseudo hypertrophy of calf muscles, shortening of Achilles tendons which results in toe walking, proximal muscle weakness which leads to frequent falls, and eventually cardiomyopathy leading to heart failure and death.

Like most DMD patients, Phyo's Achilles tendons were short, which made him walk on his toes. To correct it, orthopedic consultation was obtained and the family agreed to a bilateral heel cord lengthening procedure. However, the father believed that after the surgery Phyo would no longer need the wheelchair. The

64 ◆ *The Healing Muse* 11

procedure went well, no complications and Phyo was able to walk flat-footed. In the follow up visit, Dr. Dan decided to start him on a steroid, to reduce muscle inflammation and slow down the disease's progress. Despite having an interpreter during this visit, the parents did not understand that steroids have side effects and that Phyo's DMD was still part of him.

The steroids caused a 26 lb. weight gain (in one year's time) which Phyo didn't like because it decreased his mobility. As a result, Phyo and his parents stopped the medication on multiple occasions. The family did not understand why Phyo was taking steroids nor what would come next from his disease. They never refilled prescriptions either.

In DMD patients, the symptoms of cardiomyopathy begin to develop in their teenage years. To assess Phyo's heart, Dr. Dan referred Phyo to a pediatric cardiologist in Syracuse and made an appointment for him. Again, because the parents didn't understand the importance of this situation and because they had some difficulty in getting to the appointment, they missed it. Another attempt to make an appointment did not happen. Over the next year, Phyo's muscles became weaker including his heart muscle. He was no longer able to stand and do daily activities without having mild chest pain. He started to develop occasional fatigue and vomiting. Finally, Phyo was seen by the cardiologist who sent him to the hospital.

Now, in this quiet family room, the father asked if Phyo's heart failure was a complication of his surgery four years ago. The doctors replied that Phyo's heart failure was not a complication, that it was how this inherited disease (DMD) would progress. The family then asked why they hadn't known anything about this if it had been diagnosed long ago. Dr. Dan was shocked. For five years, he thought he had been discussing the nature of the disease with the family through an interpreter. Now he realized that the message had never been received. This family did not know that DMD was inherited, incurable, and eventually would lead to heart failure and death.

How could this happen? Well, later Dr. Dan found out that the interpreter was not relaying the entire story to the family because of cultural reasons: the interpreter did not tell the family the entirety of the diagnosis because he was afraid they would be disappointed. The job of a medical interpreter is to translate everything that the doctor says without addition or omission. Although he did not intend to cause harm, Phyo's interpreter broke this professional code. As a result, the parents never understood the magnitude of the disease and consequently had undermined the treatments including steroid and heart medications.

In Burmese culture, it is common that the caretakers or the guardians of the patients hide medical information from their loved ones to protect them from depression and feelings of hopelessness. People believe that the will to live is essential for life and without it, patients will die sooner. In fact, when Phyo's parents realized that their son did not have much longer to live, they decided not to tell him because they did not want him to feel hopeless. Perhaps this explains why the interpreter didn't relay all the information to the parents. On the other hand, it is also possible that he himself didn't understand the full spectrum of the disease. Phyo's case is an example where communication failed due to language, cultural, and educational barriers among health care providers, patients, and caregivers.

At their last meeting with the physicians, the heartbroken family agreed to take Phyo home and to follow up with palliative care. Despite their sorrow and frustration, the family was grateful for the care Phyo received and thanked everyone who took care of Phyo with compassion. Over the next two months, Phyo had a great time with his family; he passed away at home peacefully.

Phyo's case reminds us to be aware of and interested in our patients' cultures, educational levels, and proficiency with English. We must also take the time to be sure that the medical interpreter is conveying all the information the patient and family need. Without good communication, we cannot truly serve our patients the way we would want to be served.

*This article was written with the permission of the parents. All names have been changed.

Susannah Loiselle ~ *Wake Up Recycling Building*

A2113

Carolyn Agee

C—
What?
C—
Chemo.
Hair.
Poison. Pain.
Malign,
malignant.
Patient—University hospital.
Poked.
Prodded.
Persecuted.
Grand rounds. No longer a name...a number...
a disease.
A little plastic bracelet.
"Would you like a warm blanket?"
What?
Frigid. Cold.
Exposed.
"Why not show all of me? Just post a picture on an online server."
And the drone of my roommate's TV...
IV...
Morphine drip.
Confessions of an English Opium Eater.
Drip,
drip,
drip,
as I try to remember who I was.
Am.
Who I am.
Before all this,
a name, a short one. Short but beautiful.

A Script, A Momentum

Oliver Rice

Empathize with it, the master molecule,
given such a script,
such staging provisos,
and so imperious a summons to direct the action.

Reflect on the vulnerabilities of nurturing
its leading players, brain, heart, lungs,
its supporting cast and crew,
out of infancy, juvenility, adolescence,

given episodes of excess and lethargy,
complaints and excitations,
ingenuities and quirks,
itself utterly human,

bringing the company at last to an opening
into adulthood, self-sustainment,
an independent momentum,
and arriving at its retreat as mentor.

Forbear with it the role of spectator
to the progress, the drift of its dramaturgy
the ensuing colorations, mutations,
under constant threat of the fatal closing.

Give It Time

David Plumb

The roof of his mouth dripped tumor
and I knew he waited too long.
The local doctors made him angry
and his sister said when the dentist tried to
fix the back tooth it simply fell out
but he wouldn't go until he had to go.
The M.D. sent him to the Albany VA
to a Doctor Macomber, the plastic surgeon who
tacked big game animal heads to his office walls.

They cut out his hard and soft palate
and the bone under his right eye
sewed the temporal muscle under the eye
to hold it in place, stretched the sternocleidomastoid muscle
under his chin and up through the side of his mouth
to replace the palate but it was hard to swallow
food because he couldn't close his mouth.

For awhile he seemed ok.
He'd take out a pile of maps and point to where he
fought in France, Chateau-Thierry, the Marne
Flash and Sound Engineers, sometimes behind enemy lines.
He kept a tiny red book that read on page one
I am an American Fighting Man.

Then the letter that said, "I'm lonely.
No one comes to see me anymore.
Not the nurses. No one."
I flew out of Syracuse on a DC 3
that bounced and rattled the clouds.
The cancer was back.

The next time I brought Susan
and when she was out of the room
I said, "That's my girlfriend.

I'm not sure if I'm in love with her."
And he said, "Give it time."

Years later I'd realize it was the most
important thing he ever said to me.
but that day, I stared across the bed
at the box of socks on the window sill.
I took them 100 miles home the week before
washed them and mailed them back.

Then I asked him if there
was anything else I could do
and he took my hand in both of his
and said, "No. Thank you for everything."
That's all he said and the American flag
on the pole outside the window
banged and flapped in the wind.

Donna L. Emerson ~ *Grandmother Mildred Belle*

Holding on to Jenny

Jenny Haust

Geese flying south for the winter of 2002 pulled me out of the house onto my front stoop where, each time, I looked up and saw how my life would be different upon their return. I imagined hearing their call in early April, when I would stand outside again, my beautiful new baby in my arms.

Autumn passed, and I struggled to maintain normal activities despite the nausea and fatigue that challenged me, but never tempered the joy of my anticipation.

"You'll turn the corner" everyone assured me. My mom called daily asking the same thing. "Are you feeling any better today?" The same conversation for months now.

The conclusion of my first trimester brought me relief, the chance of another miscarriage reduced significantly. The twelve-week mark was my milestone, and I nurtured myself to make it to that point. It had been early February that I learned my first pregnancy would end in a miscarriage at seven weeks.

Now, December 20, I was fighting back nausea in my kitchen as I baked cookies for Steve's Christmas party. This simple tradition was something I could keep for myself, something I could accomplish. I stared at my mixer as the beaters went around and around.

Then, as I scraped dough off the beaters with a spatula, I felt as if the baby was jumping rope. I put my right hand on my stomach and felt the baby lurch. After a minute or two, I felt nothing.

I put my right hand back on my stomach and stood very still. Nothing. Leaving everything on the counter, I walked into the sunroom to lie on the couch. In the quiet, I turned from side to side trying to entice movement from my baby. A kick, a roll, anything from my baby. After several minutes, I headed into the kitchen. The doctor told me to have candy or juice to help the baby become more active if I ever felt worried about the lack of movement. I grabbed a Snickers bar, tore off the wrapper and gobbled it, washing it down with apple juice. The cookie batter was still sitting in the mixer. The flour, sugar and measuring cups were all a mess on the counter. As soon as I felt the baby move I would come back to it.

I laid my hand on my belly, began moving it around. The only thing I felt was the beat of my own heart.

"God, let everything be ok," I said out loud. My beagle, Maude, sleeping next to me on the couch, perked up her head. "I'm scared," I told her.

I picked up the phone and called Steve. "I don't feel the baby moving."

"Did you eat a candy bar or drink some juice?"

"Yes! And Steve . . . I don't feel the baby moving."

"Call the doctor's office," he said.

I told Dr. Randolph's receptionist what had happened.

"Can you come right in?"

"I will be right there," I whispered.

I grabbed my pink fleece jacket, pulled it on and quickly got into the car for the twenty- five-minute drive. It was bitter cold, but I could feel the warmth of the winter sun on my face as I passed the NYS fairgrounds on Route 690. We had not had our first snow yet. I talked to myself out loud all the way there. "Everything is fine, don't worry. Please God, let everything be all right. The baby is just fine."

I could feel my heartbeat in my throat. The steering wheel felt slippery with sweat from my hands.

Laura, Dr. Randolph's nurse, saw me immediately. She put the Doppler on my belly. It was cold. I kept wiping my sweaty hands on my pants. I was waiting to hear that rapid heartbeat I had been hearing for months now. But there was nothing. Complete silence. Laura moved the Doppler all around my belly as I lay on the table and watched her face.

"I'm going to get Catherine, the nurse practitioner. I will be right back," Laura said. All I could hear was the buzz of the fluorescent light and the crunching sound of the paper on the examining table as I moved.

Laura came back with Catherine, and after several attempts, Catherine whispered, "I can't find the baby's heartbeat." She took the sonogram device, put it on my belly and turned the monitor on. I turned my head to watch the computer screen. I could see the tiny head, body, hands and feet. Nothing moved.

"Do you want me to call Steve?" Laura asked.

"I will call him," I replied.

She took me to Dr. Randolph's quiet office, walked around to his side of the desk and picked up the phone to bring it to me as I sank in the chair. I dialed Steve's cell phone. It was painful to touch the numbers.

"Hello? Hello? Daint?" he said.

"I'm at the doctor's office and they can't find the heartbeat."

"I'm on my way."

I handed the phone to Laura and stared at the wall.

Steve arrived about an hour later, and Laura gave us directions to a radiology office in Fayetteville. She told Steve that after we went to the Fayetteville office we would need to go to St. Joseph's Hospital as soon as possible. I could barely get out of the chair.

I kept my head down as we walked out.

Steve helped me into the car and shut the door. I watched him walk around to the driver's side. I felt completely outside of myself. We drove in silence to Fayetteville. I could not speak. I just stared out the passenger side window.

Driving up Route 5, we passed a small pond where geese had gathered. The sun was still shining. The water shimmered in the light and the feathers of all the geese shone like beautiful silk.

I tried not to make eye contact with anyone when we entered the small office. The receptionist told me to sit down and said they would be right with us. I was a mess, my eyes swollen and my body tense. A woman sat with her teenage daughter in the waiting area. She saw me wiping my eyes and nose.

In a dark room the radiologist and a small group of residents scrutinized the sonogram. The silence was broken when the radiologist confirmed my baby had died. How was I ever going to get off the table?

Steve took me by the arm and lifted me. I needed to use the restroom. It was one big room with a toilet. I closed the door behind me and clicked the lock. Then, I fell to my knees. There, on that sticky tile floor, I lay down my head and sobbed.

Finally, I opened the restroom door and stared into the eyes of the woman with her teenage daughter from the radiology office.

"Can we do anything for you?"

I shook my head no.

"We are so very sorry," the mother said.

Back on 690, driving home to pick up clothing, I looked out the window towards Onondaga Lake and my silence turned into hysteria. I felt like jumping out of the car. I banged my hands on the dashboard. I screamed and cried.

"Please calm down," Steve begged.

"Call my mom; please, call my mom."

As I opened the door to the house, Maude jumped with excitement at seeing me. I walked upstairs and filled a bag with a toothbrush, my glasses, contact lens solution and hairbrush.

We arrived at St. Joseph's and took the elevator up to the labor and delivery floor.

"I need your license for identification," the nurse said.

An identification band was put on my wrist, and I was shown to a private room. It was like a cave, no windows. Only a bed and rocking chair.

I changed into a hospital gown and threw my pink fleece jacket over me.

"Hi. I'm Sean Baker. I will be the physician caring for you," said a tall, curly-haired man in a white coat. I am very sorry for your loss. Typically, under these conditions, we will induce as in a normal pregnancy. You will deliver your baby vaginally."

"Why? Why must I be awake to deliver my baby? I want to be put under," I pleaded.

Dr. Baker assured me this was the healthiest way for my body not only now, but going forward. He informed me the staff would start the typical birthing induction drugs and I would deliver the baby at some point over the next twenty-four hours.

"We need to know if you are going to want an autopsy." Dr. Baker asked. Steve and I stared at each other.

"I'll give you some time to talk about it," he said.

We decided that we did want an autopsy, an explanation for the death of our baby.

I shivered from the drugs and held tight onto my pink fleece jacket, the one thing that was not part of the sterile hospital environment.

My mom and dad cried when they saw me. I put my hand over my mouth and could not speak. I wondered how I would ever feel normal again. The thought of carrying a dead baby inside of my body made me feel sick. Knowing I had to deliver the baby naturally made it even worse. Disgusting.

"This is very difficult. Losing a baby takes a heavy toll on not only you as an individual, but also as a couple," Dr. Baker said.

Years later I would come to understand what he meant.

"Do you know what the sex of the baby is?" my nurse, Margaret, asked.

"No. We planned to wait."

Steve's parents arrived by late afternoon. Steve asked them to feed Maude and let her out. I did not want anyone around me.

Steve and I talked about what to name our baby. We decided that if we had a son we would name him Steve and if we had a daughter we would name her Jenny

Margaret sat next to me. "There is another question I need to ask. Would you like to hold the baby?"

"No," I said immediately.

Margaret looked surprised. I told Steve he should make the decision for himself.

"Jenny, you should really think about holding the baby," Margaret said. "It might give you some closure."

I began to imagine the birth. What would I do? Would I actually never see my baby? The more I thought about it, the more I felt the need to hold my baby.

Dr. Baker came to tell me his shift had ended. He said to call him if I needed anything and his partner, Dr. Colette, would take good care of me.

I clung to my pink jacket for warmth and fell in and out of sleep, waking to see my mom in the rocking chair under the dim light while Steve slept on a cot in the corner.

Later, I woke up soaking wet.

"Your water broke," the nurse said.

My mom jumped up and helped tend to me. It was 2 a.m.

"Steve, wake up!" my mom yelled.

When he did not wake, she went over and shook him.

"I feel like I need to push," I said, panicking.

The nurses quickly set up the delivery equipment.

"Where is the doctor?" I yelled.

The room was dark. The only light came from a large light the staff had wheeled in to assist the doctor in delivery. Everyone was half asleep.

At 2:34 a.m. my daughter, Jenny Rebecca was born. She weighed 1.4 pounds. The nurse wrapped her tightly in a little blanket and handed her to me. All I could see was her tiny face. It was beautiful. She was blond with little blond fuzz on her face. She was angelic. I stared at her and wept.

"Mom, do you want to hold her?" I asked. She cried as she took Jenny from Steve. Then, I held my baby again.

"Please hold her for as long as you need," the nurse said. And so I did. I studied her. I carefully unfolded the blanket from around her tiny fragile hands. I stared at her so that I would never forget her face. Finally, with one last kiss, I handed my baby to the nurse.

The next morning, the nurse asked how I was doing. I wanted to scream, "How do you think I am doing?" She asked if I wanted to be moved to the post delivery area. I could hear a woman in labor screaming from down the hall. This added to my fury.

"I want to go home," I told the nurse.

My brother had taken the first flight he could from Florida and brought me a little white ceramic snowman filled with flowers, Christmas greens and fragile Christmas bulbs. It looked tiny in his hands.

The nurse asked if I needed any medication to help calm myself.

"No."

This was not the time to mask my feelings with drugs. I needed to feel my grief.

The nurse informed me that if I felt well, I would be discharged by lunchtime. As the nurse went over general information before discharge, I saw her mouth moving, but I heard nothing.

I sat in a wheelchair, waiting to be taken to meet Steve at the main entrance, when a volunteer arrived. We did not speak in the elevator. When the doors opened to the decorated lobby, I realized the Christmas holiday that I had loved was now forever changed.

She pushed me through the lobby to the pick up area. As the exit door automatically swung open, a rush of cold air hit me. I wrapped my pink jacket tighter around me. Cold, weary and overwhelmed, I felt empty. At my lowest point, the volunteer came around the chair, and, for a long moment, gazed deeply into my eyes. She laid her brown hand on my arm and whispered "God bless you." With these words came a sense of calm. Something in her presence, her kindness, her voice had begun to heal me. I was certain then, as I watched her wheel the chair away that I would return to St. Joseph's Hospital. Next time, I would leave with a baby in my arms.

Karen Kozicki ~ *A Chair*

Prayer for Rachel

Linda Loomis

You asked for prayer.
I went to the orchard,
closed my fingers around warm fruit,
twisted, pulled, and placed
Cortlands tenderly into the basket,
hefted and bore it home.

> *O God of heavenly powers, by the might of your command*
> *you drive away from our bodies all sickness and all infirmity;*

You asked for prayer.
I stood in my kitchen,
silver knife peeling crimson skin,
slicing thin wedges into blue bowl.
Two circles of supple dough
cradling apples in Pyrex pan.

> *Be present in your goodness with your servant,*
> *that her weakness may be banished and her strength restored;*

You asked for prayer.
I made you pie,
autumn apple dredged in sugar,
fragrant with cinnamon,
essence of Moses' holy oil,
nutmeg and clove to awaken the appetite.

> *and that, her health being renewed, she may bless your holy Name;*

You asked for prayer.
I knelt before the oven door,
curved my cushioned hands
around the scorching dish,
lifted it up for you.
An offering. A doxology.
A pie.

> *through Jesus Christ our Lord. Amen.*

*From the Book of Common Prayer 1979

Album

Valerie Wohlfeld

Grandma named her Ruzsa, Hungarian for Rose.
The scrapbook's black-curtained stage:
Grandma dies but in the photo she still holds a rose.
Ruzsa dies even as the rose does not die: the living page's

beautiful lie. Ruzsa would not be good,
she pounded her fists to blood-red pith's color of roses.
Ruzsa lost her teeth: mouth like an ancient deity of riddled wood.
In Hospital, Mother brings me a rose

the nurses cannot let me hold. Doctors draw
a chart to show illness is passed along in evolution:
alongside the iris-eye's blue-blink lazuli, I saw
I was the same as Ruzsa; each revolution

in the womb uncounted; each daughter
a rose born out of a place of broken water.

Babylon

Valerie Wohlfeld

The hoarse god is all flame:
to every madness a different Babylon is given, saved.
Aside the sword, Joan of Arc knew her rocking horse's nursery name.
Between the icon and the image comes the mummy's grave.

What pure democracy
in madness given, to the pauper as to the queen.
And each Christ goes barefoot longing for the sea
and the walking on water, and the heat of Nazarene.

To hold congress with dragons and angels!
To sit with ancient deities in the dayroom.
In heaven as in hell
is the union with the bridegroom;

even the devil has his beau.
In madness as in drowning—all is the letting go.

Greggy

—*A Memoir*

Jack Tourin

On September 17, 1980, my son, Gregory Mark Tourin, died. He was seventeen.

The usual outpourings of sympathy after such an event were somewhat muted. A few close friends commiserated deeply and sincerely, but others were more restrained. Some stated openly what they thought, while others implied it.

The thought was always the same: "How can any parent mourn the death of a severely handicapped child, a child with nothing to look forward to? They should be glad it's all over."

Well-meaning people would say to my wife and me, "It's a blessing, really." Or "Your seventeen years of sacrifice are over. Now, you can live for yourselves." They failed to see the other side of this coin of sacrifice.

What mattered to us wasn't what we did for him, but what he did for us.

Greggy was born severely mentally disabled. He also had cerebral palsy. He spent most of his life in a wheelchair. During the last five years of his life, he was almost completely immobile. The only parts of his body he could move were his toes and wrists. All the natural functions of life that others accomplished automatically had to be done for him. Yet watching this child struggle to gain satisfaction, saluting each day with wide-eyed wonder at what was to come, drinking in and enjoying the tiny portion of life that was allotted to him, gave us a reward that can't be measured in normal human terms.

Taking care of Greggy was a twenty-four hours a day job. He was a very demanding child because the only means he had of controlling his life was his voice, which he used constantly. He learned to baby talk when he was five and baby-talked for the rest of his life. During all that time, we never heard from that baby talk one word of self pity or bewailing his fate.

What we did hear were demands to see, do, and go.

Greggy wanted to see everything, go everyplace, and learn everything he could. His world was restricted to a far smaller portion than that given to most people, but that tiny share of life was a constantly unfolding vista of wonderment for him.

He could read signs and large advertisements long before any teacher attempted to teach him. We discovered this when we were going through the yellow pages of the telephone book with him. There he was, calling out the names of the companies that had the larger ads. The finer subtleties of reading always eluded him, but he was able to determine that the larger sign with the big red logo meant K-Mart and the one with the circles meant something else.

When life wasn't interesting to him, it was funny.

When I became cross with him, he would say, "Daddy get mad," his eyes sparkling with anticipation, so I would wave my arms, pretending to be wildly furious. This brought a deep, heartfelt, natural, all-encompassing burst of laughter from him. No one but a mother or father can understand how it feels to hear that delirious sound of pure innocent joy. Beatrice and I would hear the same happy sound when we acceded to his request of "Mommy and Daddy dance!"

Once, when we were driving and he was in the front seat next to me, I said, "Greggy, if you say one more word or make one more sound, I'm going to throw you right out that window. Understand? One sound and out you go!"

He looked at me with an impish grin for a moment and then blurted at me, "Baaaaaaah!"

My wife and I sang to Greggy constantly. He memorized many of the simpler songs. During his last two years, he sang himself to sleep every night. He woke each morning laughing and demanding to savor more of life.

His favorite place to go was our local shopping mall, where he liked to look in the store windows and ask us to buy him things. He knew we couldn't buy him everything he asked for, but he seemed to enjoy just saying the words. In his own way, he was improving his vocabulary and his reading.

On the morning of his death, at one o'clock, on his way to the hospital emergency room, Greggy asked to be taken to the mall. We had no idea that he had only a few hours to live. We were on our way to get the cough and congestion in his chest relieved so he'd be able to sleep. He had had worse chest colds than this and had always recovered quickly.

Whether Greggy realized that he was dying we'll never know because he was cheerful and funny right to the sudden end. However, I've always suspected that he knew a lot more than we ever dreamed was possible. If he did know that he was going to die, then he had decided to finish his life as he had pursued it, developing what he had to the fullest and learning what it was possible to learn right up to his last breath.

After the funeral and the departure of our friends, Beatrice and I returned to our strangely silent house. Our friends were wrong. It wasn't over. It will never be over until my wife and I are gone and the last echoes of his singing, his laughter, and his constantly curious voice are buried with us.

For six days, I sat in the living room and cried. At the height of my agony, I made some wildly emotional decisions. I was going to quit my teaching job. I was going to retire from life. I would never smile or laugh again.

As I sat there struggling with my grief, many unusual questions came to me. One of them was, What would Greggy have done in a situation like this, if one or both of us had died before him? He would have missed us deeply, but he wouldn't have buried himself in a morass of self-pity. He would have continued to use whatever limited ability he possessed to develop, to learn, and to drink his tiny cup of life to the fullest.

To honor Greggy's memory, I decided to do what he would have done: study, learn, teach, and use my life in the best way possible.

After my son was gone, I was never able to recapture his closeness by sitting in my chair and weeping. However, over the years, when I looked into the eyes of some of my students and saw a look of magical curiosity or a sparkling sense of humor, a strange thrill went through me. I knew that for that one heavenly suspended second I had looked again into the eyes of Greggy.

Pamela Ferris-Olson ~ *In a Dutch Garden*

Visit from the Therapy Dog

June Frankland Baker

Bedded for days
in the hospital pillows
of weakness and IVs,
I was ready for a visit
from any blithe spirit who cared
to cross over, even such as this—
small, hair over eyes, jittery
paws clicking on the hard floor.
I reached over my bedside
to stroke his head.

Like pain, he wriggled away from
being touched, being still.
The Mom and Pop owners
tried all the tricks
dogs are known for—sit, catch—
but he had forgotten
his Therapy Dog lessons—
perhaps too excited
in this limbo of strange smells,
prone survivors.

That night, a shadow
haltingly approached, nudged
my waiting hand.
The light breath of memory
seemed to rest on my knee—
just as the dog I knew
a lifetime ago used to comfort,
remind me of that old ritual
of accepting,
and of giving back.

Mind Matters

Craig W. Steele

—One of the goals of psychotherapy is to make a person aware of his inner feelings at a conscious level.

—Arthur Lerner, *American Journal of Nursing.* August 1973;73(8):1336.

We romanticize the heart: it's warm or cold; gold or black;
soft or hard; aching or cheating; whole or broken. But
it's the brain that holds, deep within
mist-gray folds, the magic of emotion: passion
borne in murky caves and sparked by unseen lightning storms
into our conscious mind, that lifelong confidant
to whom the brain entrusts
our heartfelt secrets.

And yet, who doesn't keep some secrets
even from themselves?

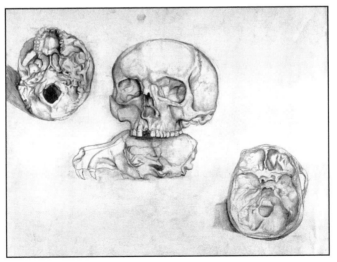

Sriharsha Gowtham ~ #1

The Dementia Unit

Susan M. Behuniak

In this place where a spoon
  refuses to reveal
  its purpose,
  every day is Monday,
  the long dead are seen while
  the living go unrecognized,
  Death stands at the exit
  so patiently
  waiting.
Forgetting is the daily pastime.

Within this charged atmosphere
  synapses strain, sputter,
  startled images
  assemble then
  dissipate,
  near misses
  tease the eyes with
  flashes of
  meaning.
The darkness darker than before.

In this place where windows
  reflect unseeing eyes,
  there are no disembodied
  smiles
  unless God is a trickster,
  a silent spectator
  to the feat of
  abandoning reason for
  rhyming.
Where memory concedes to now.

Don't Look Back

Christopher Stark Biddle

I am looking in the side mirror, and out of the glare of a setting sun I see this big white SUV and a country club blue hair waving at me to move on and holding a cell phone with a dog in her lap. I am sitting at a T intersection and what I know and she doesn't is that there is a big red pickup truck coming down on the left and I would have been splattered like a pumpkin the day after Halloween.

It is one of those white-sky March days with no pattern to it and I am feeling trapped like a fish in a net at this intersection. Plus, little things detonate me these days so I reach out and give her the finger. Then she drifts forward and bangs the back of my Chevy. Just a light tap but enough to bounce me forward an inch. So I lose it and return the favor with a little backward caress of my own and I see her head jerk forward like a bird pecking at a worm. At that point it dawns on me that we have all the makings of a disaster and I need to get out of there. My guess at this point is that Ms. Tight-Ass Road-Rage has no doubt hung up on her stockbroker and is now dialing her lawyer.

I am running over these thoughts as the traffic keeps flowing when there is tap on the passenger window and I look through the window at the face of an older lady with blue-misted hair. Damn if she is not smiling at me. Of course I find this confusing since most women would not get out of their car at an intersection and come up to some guy in a beat-up Chevy who has just given her the finger. Plus the fact that she is smiling which seems a bit weird and I begin to wonder if this is a smile or some grimace of homicidal malice. The thought crosses my mind that she might be holding a gun since I had read in *USA Today* that lots of women these days were taking pistol lessons. It also occurs to me that the sort of women who take pistol lessons are the sort of women who deep down want to shoot some man in the testicles for the fun of it and so when they tap on your window after you have given them the finger it may be best to accelerate out of there.

So at this awkward moment, my dog that is asleep in the passenger seat wakes up and he sees this women and he starts barking and slathering at the window so that it steams up. The predicament is that if I roll down the window, the dog may jump into this gal's face. Then, with all the barking my son who is in the back seat wakes up and says "What the fuck!" and I say, "Don't talk like that" and then I tell the dog to shut up and a reasonable amount of quiet ensues. But then she taps a second time and at that point my son who is 16 going on somewhere between 12 and 25 says to me "What did you do, Dad?" which requires a longer explanation than I want to give plus the implication that I have screwed up. So I don't answer knowing full well he will ask again in 3 seconds which he does and knowing full well that he would be just delighted to hear his old man had given the finger to a blue hair.

But all I can do is to roll down the window and of course the first thing I say is a lie, which is "It was a mistake" at which point she says "Don't you remember me?" and I get this wave of dizziness since things are unfolding faster than I can process and none of it seems to make sense. I look carefully at her face and her clothes that are about the same as any other suburban blue hair. The be-bop nose, the tan beach skin, the lacquered lips and the sharp gray eyes that are tough because behind them lies the cash that can flatten you. She is wearing the predictable gray cashmere sweater, a little blue scarf, some pearls and funny little silver earrings in the shape of saddle stirrups. At first I thought a memory might blossom but nothing unfurls. And so I say "No, Madam." The "Madam" is for politeness to defuse the situation and alleviate any later accusation that I have been a jerk. And then she says, "Are you sure?" and she keeps smiling and I sense we are playing a game. Then my son pipes up and he is speaking to me in his grown-up 25 year old voice and he says, "It's Mrs. Duquesne, Dad."

And then I am rescued because she says "The hospice, for Janet. About 3 months ago," and my heart thump thumps and my mind starts to go in a direction I do not want it to. Though the memory is still coagulating, I do remember the hospice. I remember the day Janet asked for the phone and she called them and asked for help. This is unfurling in my mind when I get this picture of a women in a pant-suit and tweed hat walking up our pavement on a white-sun day and knocking on our door and the bulb flicks on and there is Mrs. Duquesne standing there giving me the same smile she was giving me then.

At this point I hear the short beep of a horn and I look back and there is a Fed Ex truck jammed up behind the SUV in high dudgeon to get by. Now my primary goal at this point is to get away from all of this confusion but I can't leave Mrs. Duquesne just standing there like a hitchhiker and so I say "Oh . . . Of course" and she says "It is nice to see you," and she looks at my son and says "How are you, Andrew?" and my son says something which I can't hear because the Fed Ex blows again. At this point, Mrs. Duquesne disappears and I see her emerge behind my Chevy like a flushed partridge and she gets back into her SUV. I feel this sudden relief since the road is now clear and so I pull forward and take a left and accelerate and I don't look back.

But then my son says "What the fuck!" in an accusatory sort of way, which makes me mad because I hate that word plus the fact that he is basically telling me in his own articulate way that I am a rude jackass. So I slam on the brakes, the tires squeal, the dog goes flying into the dashboard, somewhere a horn blares and I veer off the road splattering gravel. My son says "What the fuck" again.

I take a long hard look at Andrew. He is a thin kid and for some reason has big ears and cuts his hair short and has a small tattoo of a lightning bolt on his neck. Today he has a cold and his nose is red and his hazel eyes are watery. Both he and the dog are looking at me as if I have just burst into flames and I am noticing the sweet metallic smell of burning brakes. I want very much to say something to him but I am not sure what it is. We are looking at each other and I can hear my breathing and I know something is going on between us. His rheumy eyes remind me of tears and I feel dizzy and tired and the anger or whatever demon it was that slammed on the brakes flies out of the window like a bat.

At this point just about the worst thing imaginable happens when I look over and see the white SUV and the little blue rimmed face of Mrs. Duquesne and, yes, she is smiling and I see she is unbuckling her seat belt and starting to get out and I am Bonnie and Clyde at the roadblock.

Mrs. Duquesne was the only hospice volunteer we had. She came about 7 or 8 times plus most of the last week. She always wore a cashmere sweater, had an emerald ring, read horse magazines, smelled of perfume and had blue bleached cotton candy hair. Maybe she was or 55 or 65 but you couldn't tell because she was carefully packaged and wore a perpetual biblical smile which seemed designed to ward off any ugly impropriety that might attempt to wedge itself into her day. She would come in and tell me about some flower show or a trip that she was planning and then she would go into Janet and give her a bath and rub her arms and legs. I could hear them talking and sometimes laughing and then long silences. And just once a moan that made me want to leave the house.

Once I heard her reading a poem about a girl that had been sucked out of the broken window of an airplane and as she fell the wind peeled off her clothes and she could feel the clouds blowing through her rotating limbs. I heard Janet saying, "That is so lovely," which seemed odd but caught me in the gut and after that I didn't listen to their conversations.

During those last 10 days or so I did all the cleaning. I would scrub and deodorize the house every day and change the sheets. For the last week it was just the 3 of us during the day waiting together and Mrs. Duquesne helping with the dinner and feeding Janet and making me promise to call in the night if there were developments. In the evening Andrew and I would play cards or read and he would spend time with Janet before going to bed and then I would crawl in beside her. She was usually asleep by then and most of our talking was over as is usually true when you have been with someone for a long time. Of course at the end she did have trouble sleeping and once she kicked the blankets off and swore and another time she sobbed for a few minutes and all I could do was to rest my hand in the valley of her hip.

On the last night Janet woke me and asked for Mrs. Duquesne. I remember she spoke so clearly and her voice was strong with authority and I thought this could not be the end because her tone was bell clear. And Mrs. Duquesne came and was with Janet for about two hours and once or twice I would go in and they were just sitting there holding hands, not talking. Janet looked so strong and healthy that I was surprised when Mrs. Duquesne came into the living room and told me she had died. It had happened quickly, there was no pain. She was so sorry that I was not there. I said that really didn't matter and thanked her for her help.

So Mrs. Duquesne is at my window and I am rolling it down with the automatic button and there is no way in God's green earth that I know what to say. I am sitting with absolutely no words on my mind like an old broken windmill and of course wishing that all this would end. I can hear Andrew snuffling and wheezing and smell the burning brakes and as the window spools down Mrs. Duquesne's blue rimmed smiling face seems to flow into the car like ink in water. I start muttering and Andrew is stuttering hello and the dog is up and bouncing around and waving his tail and then there is a book being handed through the window. And then the window is spooling up and Andrew and I are sitting together and he is thumbing the book open to a creased page and a stalk of forsythia is dropping down into his lap.

I imagine that Mrs. Duquesne lives in a stone house with a circular driveway. There is a fountain in the center of the lawn and the steps to the house are marble with box bushes in planter boxes on either side that will be taken into the nursery in the winter. When you come into Mrs. Duquesne's hallway you look through double doors to a piano in the distance and a sloping lawn beyond that. In Mrs. Duquesne's house there is a library to your left and a dining room to your right and there are always cocktails and quiet conversation. I try to think of Mrs. Duquesne coming in from the lawn and walking toward me. She passes by the piano and through the double doors but then she disappears and so I start her walking again with no success. Sometimes I try from the side thinking perhaps she is in the library and reading a book and she will hear the bell and get up and move with decorum into the vestibule but then she always disappears. I tried once and only once to think of her lying in bed under a thick white down comforter. She is reading a book but I can't see the title and she is falling asleep but I can't see her eyes.

On that last night Mrs. Duquesne did the dishes. It was the first time I had seen her hands at work. She had very thin wrists and long fingers that curled around the glasses like seaweed and she moved her arms like a conductor, organizing and scrubbing and drying. I remember looking at those hands that had held Janet's and wondering what memories they possessed. I wonder if you can dream when you die? Do you dream of fingers relaxing and slipping apart or of poems you have read or perhaps of being born?

I never did ask her the question. Perhaps there was not much of an answer but I do speculate. I can hear quiet breathing and see the veins on the back of her white hand. My thumb—or is it Mrs. Duquesne's—lies across the top of her wrist and the pulse is steady. The sheets of the bed are cool against our arms and there is a distant hovering of lavender in the air. The book is open across her chest and rises and falls as she breathes. And she must be dreaming of the forsythia in the yard and of running through the grass with her son and perhaps of being a bird and then of falling through the sky and shedding shreds of satin, velvet and cotton that bloom up behind her like a meteorite of glory. What haunts me is that instant of transition, that slipping behind the cloud, that infinitely tiny moment of vaporous time. That was taken away from me.

All that is something Mrs. Duquesne has kept to herself.

Donna L. Emerson ~ *Cabaña*

Karen Kozicki ~ *Berlin Wall Panel, The Intrepid, NYC*

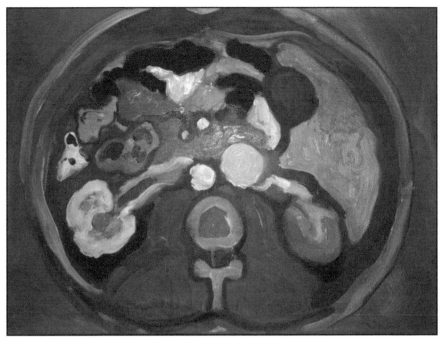

Zofia Nowicki ~ *CT3*

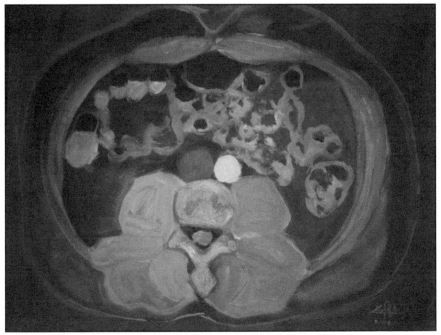

Zofia Nowicki ~ *CT4*

Elegy

Claudia M. Reder

My mother grows too close
        to the house, emitting a burst
of heat on the glass
        like the yawn of a large
speckled cat
        ready to nap.
I forgive her need to thread
        her roots in this
uncertain earth. Riga, 1939,
        the table set for dinner,
the family simply walked out
        of the house
towards America.

        So, let the aromas
of foods she loves circulate
        to the tips of her leaves.
Let her anxieties nest.
        As we both age,
learning how to be plus size
        in a petite world,
as German accents disappeared
        from the neighborhood,
instead of 'Oy' my friend jokes 'Ai,'
        let this tree honor stillness
of dry summer nights
        the way new snow refreshes
indolent winter.
        At the heartwood
I catch my breath,
        Against her tilted
and muscular trunk
my husband
        and I toast with a glass of dry wine,
he parses the orb of an orange,
        hands me one manageable
slice at a time.

Mrs. Bean Fighting Mad At Me

Elinor Cramer

Why all this fuss about Lee?
I don't want him to come;
you didn't tell me.

The aide was smearing goo on me,
I couldn't come to the phone.
Why make such a fuss about Lee?

I won't see him. Then where will you be?
Just because I'm in Dunham Home,
you don't ask me?

You with your cake and strawberries.
I had a birthday in June,
but you make this fuss for Lee,

and just do what you please—
what's it like?   You-with-a-place-of-your-own.
Tell me. You tell me.

Lee's got an apartment and Jo Jo kitty,
you took my cat to a farm.
Why all this fuss about Lee?
You tell me. You tell me!

Throughout Life

Andrea Hsue
Dearing Writing Award, Poetry
Student Division

Under the advance and retreat of shadows cast by clouds you stand
Your own shadow marking the generosities of the sun . . .
First the bud toughened through trial—
    wartime service
    taking any job to survive
    four children sharing one pair of shoes
    The Great Depression.

Soon it saw fertile soil—
    An observant eye
    A reflective mind
    Eagerness to learn
        Upturnings of the soul by the beauty of poetry
            With Irish homily,
            Welsh writing,
            A prayer: "Thy sea is great, our boats . . . so small."

Then came the rain—
    The rapid yet wearying travel of years—
    Time pooling like water
    Pain spilling it out in tears
        The wife you loved, the most beautiful girl you'd ever seen, obscured in
            shadow and anger.
        Alzheimer's burrowed a pit of anger so deep that her outbursts of hostility
            could not express all of it.
    Rushing waters of loss.
Roots breathed sharply, clinging to faith that God saw the broken heart.

Finally, warmth by the sun—
    Your eyes danced by finding the radiance of
        a hand tapping to music, or
        a "you ok?"

from what had seemed to be an empty shell
Light bursting forth.
Assumptions burning away by the flares of awakening
    in your hallmates with dementia.
Do you see it?
Leaves unfolding to receive the revelation of the dignity
    that always remains in the human soul.

Kathleen Gunton ~ *Sun in a Flower*

Finding a Copy of *Out of Africa* (published 1938)

Heidi Nightengale

I felt at first sight of it, like understanding
the mysterious ministrations of a church, and
stayed a long time alone before bringing
down the news. I rested like the trunk
among the piles of black walnuts
fallen through the roof of the barn.

He had pushed himself through the gene carrying
memory to leave a granddaughter,
firstborn of firstborn daughters,
the first edition to replace the paperback
that had served me as a saving place for dreams
of my own farm one day—
a farm for wildflower seeds mixed among the coffee.

And *yes* I thought; Africa had remembered him,
and he had left the book packed in a trunk for me to find
when I was twice the age he ever got to be.

Undercover Agent

Annita Sawyer

In 1960, as I approached seventeen-years-old, I began to act seriously depressed and suicidal. Over the next six years, I was placed in one hospital and then another. I've since become a clinical psychologist. This is part of a memoir from that period.

April 1967

One morning, a few months into college, I was on my way to the library, when I stopped for a moment on the sidewalk at Broadway and 116th Street, just outside the large iron gates that marked the entrance to the Columbia College campus. Blossoming fruit trees perfumed the air; their scattered white petals made lacy patterns on the ground. The whole area bustled with chattering students and rattling cars rushing past each other up and down the hill. Despite the morning's chill, my blouse felt warm from nervous sweat. I shifted my stack of books and freed a hand to tuck a loose wisp of hair behind my ear. I wanted to compose myself, to make sure that I looked normal.

I noticed an attractive, curly haired girl walking toward me.

"Hey, Annita, what are you doing here?" She was smiling. She sounded enthusiastic.

"Hi!" I replied with a big grin. I scanned her face and searched my brain for any indication that I'd seen her before, while I prayed for divine intervention and hoped that my pause wasn't lasting too long. *Dear God, who is she?*

"What have you been up to?" I ventured. By now I was feeling disembodied, like a robot reciting a script. But I'd won acclaim for my acting in high school, so I pulled myself together and focused on my part. I took a deep breath—*no sweat stink yet*—and grinned again.

She dived into a report on her recent activities. She shared an apartment in the Village and dated musicians and MBAs, but there was no one special yet. After college she had taken a year off and lived in France. Now she worked in a bank downtown at a job she didn't like. She was there to check out the law school. She paused for a moment. "You?"

"It's been a while, hasn't it?" I responded as if I were answering her question, as if we were old friends. She returned to talking about herself, and whenever she looked for something from me I produced sympathetic phrases that encouraged her to continue. "Yeah? . . . No kidding . . . He didn't! . . . " What looked like a conversation might have qualified, in essence, as a monologue.

Like any experienced undercover agent, I was buying time while I gathered strategic information. My concealed identity: former mental patient, returned to the world now six years out of step, with almost no memory of life outside an institution. My public persona was congenial local college student—I had just started at Columbia's School of General Studies. I matched my responses to my friend's emotional tone as I noted her age, her dress, and her choice of words. She looked as if she was about my age. I was almost twenty-four, but I looked younger, which meant age alone wasn't enough. She wore an ironed green corduroy skirt with a clean white cotton blouse and a pretty sweater. Her speech flowed easily and had a nice rhythm. She was lively. No tics, dishevelment, or ghostlike transparency, which would have suggested someone from the hospital. Most likely she had gone to my high school.

Confessing my ignorance was not an option. If I told someone I had lost most of my memory, I would have to explain why. If I said it was due to loads of shock treatments in a mental hospital, the person likely would run as fast as possible in the other direction. No one would choose to destroy her social acceptability with psychiatric revelations if she could avoid it. And people who had known me before the hospital couldn't believe I had forgotten so much—especially who they were.

I had seen the dismay on faces of those I told before I knew better. Awkward and fumbling, thinking I had to be honest, I had explained that I had no awareness at all of experiences they were certain we'd shared. I figured my classmates knew about my hospitalization, since I had left school suddenly and never returned. Certainly Sara and Sue, my best friends, knew. And kids talked—nothing in high school stayed secret for long.

A few of my friends had looked particularly alarmed, angry even. They tried not to show they were upset with me, but their skin flushed and their eyes bugged out. My guess was that they thought I didn't consider them important enough to remember. Others might have worried I was truly insane, although no one said anything directly. They seemed really nervous around me—stammering, fidgeting, beating around the bush. And how could I blame them? In those encounters I stammered as badly, if not worse, than they did.

I first realized how delicate a situation my forgetting could be a few years earlier when my brother's best friend Bobby came by while I was home from the hospital on a pass. Bobby rang the bell, and I let him in. I asked him to wait while I went to find Richie, who was home on a pass from the Army. Soon after that they left to go drinking. My brother didn't return until after I was asleep. But the next day, before I went back to the hospital, a scowling Richie stopped me in the front hall. He pushed his face into mine. He glared into my eyes.

"I'm very disappointed in you," Richie said, pointing his finger at me as if I were some snot-nosed kid and not his older sister. "I expect you to treat my friends with respect, do you understand?"

"Wha-what?" I stammered.

"Bobby said you were cold," Richie growled. "You acted like you didn't know him."

"He's your friend. I wasn't rude."

Then I learned that Bobby and I had been friends, too. He had been looking forward to visiting with me as well as with Richie. I could see why he'd felt rejected when I assumed he was interested only in my brother. I apologized. But I was also disappointed. I had thought my brother understood my memory problem. I was glad that I was about to leave.

Maybe a year later, just after Thanksgiving, I was visiting home again. Richie had come home, too, although that day he was in New York City with friends. I had been out of the hospital for a few months, working as a bookkeeper at a hosiery company, living at the Y. During the years I had been away, my friends had graduated from high school and gone to college. They were moving on with their lives. My brother, who was very social and could get along with anyone, had become good friends with Lynnie, my childhood best friend. She had moved to California and married, but this week she was visiting her old home town.

On that chilly November day, when Lynnie stopped over to see my brother, I didn't recognize her. She looked flustered, too. A great deal of time had passed since our best-friend days of elementary and junior high school. Also, she may have been worried about what to do with a possible nut case.

"Annita, wow, uh, how's it going?"

By then I knew enough to act like we were friends. "You look great. It's been a while," I said. "Can I get you some juice?"

"What a treat!" Lynnie's face lit up. "When was the last time? Remember those sleepovers we used to have? And the games! Do you still play?"

"Richie is in New York. He told me you might be over . . . Yeah, I'm good, uh, how's it with you? . . . I can't believe how cold it is . . . Last week wasn't so bad . . . ."

Lynnie looked beautiful in an up-to-date, stylish way. I stared at her green wool hat, at her clothes, but especially at her face as she brought up stories of old times together: " . . . we went to the beach with your mother and decided to go to that party without asking . . . remember? When your brother took your books . . . Remember? . . . how we hated dancing school. . . Don' t you remember?"

I had nothing to say. Lynnie sat on the couch and fiddled with her hat.

My face burned, and I began to sweat. I looked as intently as I dared. My ears examined every word. Inside my brain I urgently reviewed my life, and still I came up empty. I couldn't remember anything about us. It was as if I had gone into my garden and found only asphalt and rocks where bright flowers and ripe vegetables were supposed to be growing.

I had no choice left but to explain. "You know I was in the psych hospital here for a few years, right?" I paused. Lynnie didn't move. "Well, they gave me lots of shock treatments. It makes you forget everything. I can't remember anything about school—elementary or high school. I hate that. I'm really sorry."

At first she looked crushed. Inhaling slowly, Lynnie seemed to consider what I had said. I watched her finely penciled eyebrows lift, questioning. She tilted her head and tightened her lips. When she finally exhaled, she sighed.

"That's good to know," Lynnie said, while her tone of voice implied that it wasn't. "Please tell your brother I was here." She picked up her purse, grabbed the jacket beside her, and left the house. I heard "Bye" a second before the door closed.

I knew Lynnie didn't believe me. I might even have scared her. After that, I hadn't seen or heard from her again.

"Have you been in touch with anyone else? Mac? Sara?"

The question brought me back. I was right: this girl in front of me was a friend from high school. Mac and Sara had been in my class. I answered her without lying, "No, not recently. What about you?"

She took off again with stories about her friends and her adventures. Eventually, I could even figure out who she was—Elaine. She'd been part of the group that shared most of the honors classes. That time I was lucky. I'd gathered enough clues to identify her by name. I didn't remember any specific incidents involving Elaine and me, but at least I knew her name.

"Well, this was fun. Tell the others 'Hi' for me when you see them."

"I sure will."

Elaine smiled, picked up her book bag, and walked away toward the street.

"See you . . . Elaine," I added, when she'd moved on too far to hear me.

Over time, I had come to realize that no one could understand my condition of missing memory. I was incomprehensible, as if I were a visitor from another planet with customs known only to myself. So I had developed a system to avoid alienating or frightening people I met. If I listened to them carefully, at some point I would hear enough about who the individual was and where he or she came from that I could figure out the context in which they used to know me. After that I'd make some reference to what I thought we must have in common, and the person would leave satisfied, grateful even.

I learned from this how hungry people were for someone to pay attention to what they had to say, and how little they noticed what actually occurred. I began to feel like an expert in listening. And, more important, in the process of seeking information to prove I was the person they thought I was, I learned a bit more about myself—who the Annita was they had known as their friend.

Yolanda Tooley ~ *Two Lights*

Kidney, Shared

Hannah Craig

Memory boot-scoots out the door.
An alien recollection of cells, fingers,
and whistled songs is held under the surface,
a wriggling, dark fish.

A ghost walks through you
when you pick up a ketchup bottle.
When you view the hormone-veiled vision
of Judith, nipples framed by strong white arms,
carrying the head of Holofernes.

But ignore that. Ignore the giant space
in the body—a spare linen closet
remodeled into a bathroom, with a
built in towel-warmer, pedestal sink.
The body rips out its own spare fabric.
Parachutes engender themselves
in the egress of faint rain,
in shadows over concrete.

You study everything missing.
All the holes and sequences of disappearance.
Children shluffed from playground to ice cream truck
to chest to grave. Brides carried to beds.
Mothers letting go,
despite the ring of fire,
emptying out.
And the crushing smell of lilac.
The apple perfume of the hospital nurse
adjusting pillows and rails, confessing heroics,
worship, faith, plainly just a good guy.

The Errant Heart

David C. Manfredi

chasing after palpitations
from scars within a weary chest
and smoke filled breaths
plucking vascular strings
rigid in their dissonance
hardened by reckless disregard

we snake a wire into its chamber
override its rebellious nature
quell the insurgent muscle
keep the uneasy peace
a device placed under the skin
senses its every peccadillo
commands obedience to its settings
jolting it back to reality
surveillance for flawed hearts . . .

all the same filled with longing
coping with sorrow
all in good rhythm
all in good perfusion

Post Sigmoid Colectomy or Here We Go Loopdy-Loo

Donna L. Emerson

Let me out of Mt. Zion before I go crazy. Let my lungs stay clear, my wounds uninfected, my heart beat normally, still capable of hope. And protect my shortened bowel, now without its loop-de-loops.

A group of women from five different countries put me to sleep, cut open my body and cut away eighteen inches of my colon. Where did they put it? I dream of it as the hydra made of water in *The Abyss*, visiting me under my bed.

They fill the rest of me with air and narcotics to make me forget that part of my body is gone.

There are no Knights of St. John at the Gates of Rhodes, only professionally trained technicians who confuse orders, drugs, mistake symptoms, and teach how a lovely mind can be ruined in just an hour. Dilaudid tastes like death.

Just push the button every time it's green, she says. So I push, feelings sentences leave me, then phrases, then words, until I pull my thumb away and say, *Stop*. Or was that my head nodding?

She begins a new drug after talking to the new resident, Topenol. Take three times only or it ruins the kidneys.

Then morphine, then Percoset, why not Nocar? Heating pads feel best, almost like a good fever, but my blood pressure's rising 196/92, so hydolozene in a hurry. Pain still not controlled.

The doctor flushes in, wears a necklace of glass squares I'd buy if she hadn't seen it first. She comes to see me on her way from Bloomingdale's because I am bleeding. We speak eleven seconds about the word "red." She likes the phrase *surgical blood* as she swishes against her tissue paper bags on the way out. She never looks at my incisions.

Do you bruise easily? The night nurse asks me at midnight. I count ten bruises on my arms. *Do you bruise easily?* Asks the 5 am nurse with the needle. I have a girdle of purple and black bruises around my waist. Double needle sticks, bruises on my incisions.

I hang on in memory to the old hospital I knew, Drs. Sylvestri, Weitzel, Erick Erickson when he taught here, flowers sent by friends, the one nurse who seems capable of still caring and diagnosing with thought instead of routine.

I walk the halls to find the San Francisco sun, her mushroom canopy clouds, clean sky devoid of H1N1, the one cleaning lady who cleans all of my room, not just the floor. The gift shop lady who's worked here for thirty years says, *Let me pick that up for you, I know how you must feel. My husband and daughter, both treated for cancer, upstairs.* We both look up.

More Heparin sticks. And glue holding "my new smile" together.

Elegy

Suzanne McConnell

Alto

She didn't know. She didn't know how to go on. She didn't know how to talk to her mother. She didn't know why it had happened. She didn't know why it had happened. They had gone to Florida. It was the first and only time they had left their children. She didn't know how she could talk to her mother, she didn't know how she could look at her, she didn't know. She didn't know how to tell the oldest, who was six. She didn't know how the baby could in one moment be sucking from his bottle, and an hour later, when her mother went in to him, her mother said, be still. She didn't know how she could ever go to the Holy Mother again, how she could ever go to the Church of the Holy Father again. She wished she'd never come to this country, to Brooklyn, everything was fine here, her husband made money, more than ever they would have in Poland, she didn't know why she'd come here. They were rich, they had more than in Poland if they worked their whole lives, they were rich enough to go to Florida. She didn't know why she'd come here.

Treble

He had asked for a puppy for a long long time and now they had given him one. He couldn't wait to show it to Marcel. Marcel was very little, much littler than him, he was six and Marcel wasn't even one.

He didn't know where Marcel was. When Mama and Papa went to Florida, his grandmother stayed with them. She made pirogis and sandwiches with bacon and spoke Polish all the time, she lived near them and she came over a lot and it was okay when Mama and Papa went. Marcel stayed home with their grandmother, while he went to school as usual. He didn't see his Papa much anyway because his Papa worked a lot. He missed his mother though, and everyday after his grandmother picked him up from kindergarten when they got home he liked to tickle Marcel. One day Marcel was gone. His mother and father came home. He had tickled Marcel too much. Once he hid him in the closet. If Marcel came back, he would give him the puppy. Everyone talked in whispers.

Baritone

He saw the piano in a loft building he was renovating. All morning he noticed it. An old upright. It was missing ivory. It had a broken hammer on the above the middle E. It was a wreck of a piano. It was named Chester.

That was his name.

At lunch, he put down his tools. He told his men they should go home. "Go home, go home!" he shouted.

He knew the men well. They looked at him, they spoke to each other. They said to him in Polish, "Let us help, we'll keep working and you go home," they said. "Holy God bless you." He didn't hear them. He told them to go. "Go! Go!" He had never yelled before.

He sat down at that piano. He banged on it. He broke keys. He wept.

Contralto

She went to church. It was dark and cool. There were a few others, here and there. She sat a long time. Then she knelt.

Father God in Heaven, she whispered. I didn't do anything, You know that. I gave him a bottle an hour before. He took it, he drank, he was thirsty, he cried a little first. Like always, like normal. If not normal, I would call the doctor, one of the numbers from the long list they gave me. I had six babies myself. I know how to take care of babies.

My daughter doesn't look me in the eye. My son-in-law either. My daughter, my Magda. I did not want to stay with the children. I confess, Father. But I say yes, I will care for the children, I am glad for you, thank you for bringing me here, you should go to Florida. And this baby is dear. He puts his little hands on my cheeks and gives me kisses on the mouth. Father. I take him a bottle at 1 o'clock. I peek in at 2:15. He is sleeping. At three again, I go. He is still. He is still, like a doll.

I know they know I didn't do anything. I know I didn't do anything. I know they know.

Not in the Spring

Charlotte F. Otten

Why do children never leave the womb?
Mine are 42 and 40 now,
and still I labor when I hear

they have the flu, or cysts on
wisdom teeth, or muscle pains high
in the chest, or rumbles in the colon.

I have a friend—their age—
with cancer in a testicle and in his
liver. I watch the chemotherapy

shrink his tough resilient frame
into a withered stalk, the kind
we cut down in the fall, not in the spring.

Three Poems

*

Though they give nothing back
they're weak and in the bargain
both eyes are overgrown

with branches, with hillsides
calling out from the dirt
that no longer knows the difference

—what they can still point to
you drink as thighs and breasts
and rainwater stroking the Earth

shaking it, almost a mouth
almost a sun, a smell
burning between, half roots

half far away, half squint
and your heart too is emptying
struggling, moist, around you.

**

Its shadow is helpless here
festering the way your fingers
lean over the watermarks

not yet covered with paper
though left in the open
this wall could heal, the butterflies

gently circling down
and under the painted leaves
the empty branches and wings

—you thin this paste
as if one arm works the other
till what you turn in

unfolds toward painful corners
and days without a sea
making room for you.

***

Hours! you walk the way this dirt
is hammered, each heel brought home
where the Earth broke apart, opened

for the sound scrapped off closed doors
and burning hair—these black shoes
need a rag soaked in moonlight, rubbed

till the shine comes from further off
spreads out, not yet a field, struggles
though each step starts with the dead

then stops, forgets how, expects one leg
to tighten the other as if every bone
thickens in the center, needs more coming in

and leaving, more dirt, more nails
—everything you touch you pull up, freed
from the afternoons, the graves, and the drift.

Dear Brain,

Perry S. Nicholas

I lost the first draft of this letter.
I wrote it while listening to someone
read a paper for twenty minutes
about Marianne Moore's snail.

Which side of you will take responsibility?
I've forgotten. Like a computer,
you anticipated *heart* as the object
of my salutation, affections, questioned
the empty space on my rough draft.

Sweet nemesis, are you lying awake
tonight on the top bunk in my room?
Close your screen, let me sleep.
I'm appalled at how you persist,
your down light bluer than night sky.

With all due respect, I'd rather
live tenderly than always on guard
and duck your stroking, analytical eye.
I suspect I am taking a risk
when I complain. Sincerely—

Your Limbic System

Kailyn McCord

My Dad and I were at La Salsa, a chain Mexican food restaurant we frequented. He said he wanted to sit down and talk, something about how I'd been doing in school, which was mediocre. He jiggled his leg under the table until our food came, smiling at me when he looked up and remembered I was there. I ate a bean and cheese burrito, tasting the staleness of the tortilla underneath the grilled crunch.

"So Kail, you know those pills I take?"

I did know the pills, little white round pills that he kept in an orange bottle on the top shelf of the medicine cabinet.

"Well, you know how I get . . . how I get too fierce sometimes?" He took a large bite of the Caesar-Fiesta salad.

"Yeah. But you haven't done that in a while."

"Those pills help me with that. I . . . I'm what they call a bi-polar two, kiddo, which means that sometimes I get a little too up or a little too down, and these pills help even me out."

"Okay."

"But it's more important than that. I wanted to tell you about it, because it seems like . . . it seems like maybe you've been a little down lately."

"Yeah. But that's okay." Black bean juice dripped down my chin.

"I know it's okay, it's totally okay." He laughed and looked down at his plate. "But I just wanted to tell you, that more than anything they do for me, this medication—it's called lithium—makes me feel more like myself. More like I can hold myself in, like I can . . . like I'm more centered. And I just want you to know, that if you ever feel like that, like . . . like scattered like that, maybe we could do something to help you out."

"I'm not taking pills."

"Having this thing, it doesn't mean anything about you as a person, or about your character. It's in the reptilian part of your brain, in your limbic system, and the pills—"

"I'm not taking pills." My burrito looked sad, sitting flat and oozing greasy cheese on the black plastic plate.

"Okay kiddo. Okay."

He took a large bite of salad and chewed with his mouth open. I stared out the window, through the grated off-patio, and watched women in spandex pants walk by with Frappuccino cups, pushing strollers and unlocking their cars with little beeper remotes. The heat lamps behind us glowed red, toasting my back and leaving my front freezing. I glanced at my father, at his drooping chin and the wild, bushy hair sprouting up from his eyebrows and down from his nostrils. The hair trembled as he looked into his salad, like cricket wings moving together every time he bounced his head. He ran over the conversation we had just had inside his mind, giving short nods and moving his lips just a little. His eyebrows reacted to nothing, and he stared into the white dressing, leftover bits of cheese and crouton glued to the bottom of the bowl.

James Loiselle ~ *Bug*

The Boat Accident

Fani Papageorgiou

Out of the cold salt water the fishermen brought up a man caught in a net and
placed him on the afterdeck
His boat, the *Maria Mancini*, had veered off nearly perpendicular to the chop
and angled to the starboard.

The fishermen looked across the water
the morning light deeper across the bay
Could be an accident, could be anything, they told each other, like
Dipping teacups into the ocean, without knowing how much water they could
carry.

In the frigid seawater, the man had not died facedown in shallow depths
We know a little about drowning, the fishermen told the coroner.

Drowned men are eaten in the face by crabs and crayfish
they feed on the softest portions, the eyelids and the lips.
This man inhaled a large volume of seawater yet his lungs are dry, the pathologist said *There are broken blood vessels in the whites of his eyes, like crunches of
spilt sugar.*

The official cause of death
Anoxia and acute disturbance to the composition of the blood
Something lodged in the tissue of the brain.

Some of us are respiratory when we hit the water, the forensic pathologist mur-
mured to himself
And the fishermen nodded.
Men, like birds, follow rivers and shorelines
Even though there is a small, hard part in each
standing back, watching his own drowning.

Sinus Iridium (Bay of Rainbows)

Mary Kathryn Jablonski

The elusive bay of rainbows
guarding the island planted with promise,
where light shines through every storm and the bow
is not a weapon but a veil of hope that shimmers
like spun sugar never touching the tongue,

creates again the place where droplets rise
in radiant hues and fuse into a blinding white called *stars*.

Hair

Howard F. Stein

Helen, one of our clinic nurses, had one head of hair. It was thick; it was wavy; it was bushy. It was everything that my balding head was no longer. Helen had been a nurse here as far back as I can remember. Her memory—of everything—was a vital skill upon which we heavily relied. She knew people, medications, phone numbers, what worked and what didn't. She was a presence as well as a role. While not exactly charismatic, she was always pleasant, even cheerful, eager to get the job done—and then some. She was a quiet leader.

Then, out of the blue, her doctor discovered breast cancer in her. Helen soon had surgery and then a regimen of chemotherapy. All the splendid hair on her head fell out. When she returned to the clinic, Helen began wearing hats to work, always tasteful, but her head was always covered. Within only a few days, everyone who worked in the clinic showed up with coverings on their heads: dressy hats, corny hats, head scarves, and of course, since this is Oklahoma, baseball caps— with the bill facing forward. Head covering became the new standard rather than the exception.

When I asked, no one could remember exactly who came up with the idea. It was as if everyone thought of it simultaneously. The hats stayed on for weeks— until Helen ceased to feel that her head was naked in the sight of everyone. Only when her hat came off did others bare their heads.

No one had words for it until I asked. Certainly no one talked of "social solidarity!" They just put on hats as if it were the obviously right thing to do under the circumstances. Her coworkers did not want her to be or feel alone, to feel different, to feel embarrassed, to feel like some kind of freak. Most of the time, it is an individual who blends in with the group. This time, it was the group who enveloped Helen in themselves, becoming, in the process, like her. She, in turn, was no different from them.

Helen is back to work full-time—with a full, thick, wavy, bushy head of hair. My memory of the sea of hats administering medical care remains an unforgettable sight I shall cherish.

Distance Grid

Howard F. Stein

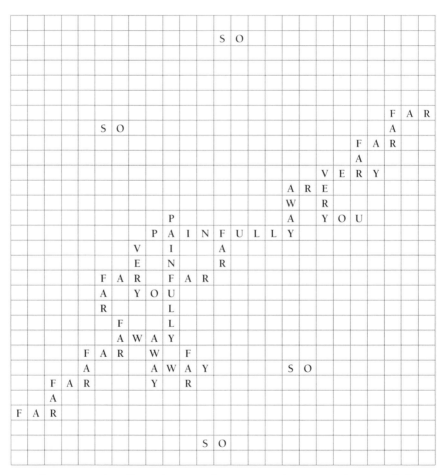

After six months of long-distance planning, email correspondence, and phone conversations, I met the person who organized the two-day medical conference at which I was, thanks to her efforts, an invited speaker. The intellectual, emotional, alnd spiritual resonance between us was instantaneous and intense. Suddenly, after two days, I was on my way back to the airport, and home half a continent away. The "grid" is a memorial to connection, separation, absence, longing, and finality. The fragmented sentence depicts my search for wholeness in the face of loss.

My Dad Waits All Year for Christmas to Come

Teresa Sutton

Winter solstice starts the hum in his body, wakes his spirit. His eyes
sharpen, lock on a ball of yarn, a cat that waits to bat it about.
Shortest day of the year, he says. Every day after this one will be
a little bit longer. Light shifts in his eyes, the yarn unravels
down to memories—muzzy, unfocused. He misses the mouse
that gnaws upon and filches a length of the alpaca.

A pot of fifteen vegetables softening in stock until a stick blender
makes a thick puree of yesterday and today, the distant and the now,
when he forgets to take his medicine or forgets to meet his brother
at the usual spot for lunch. When Christmas comes, he rushes
through the day waiting for his chance to head home early, to drive in the light
plus a dozen other excuses to leave. Years ago, he confided
that my mother's ghost comes; her mouth moves, but he can't discover
what she's trying to say. The sound is mute; the button, depressed
on the remote. His memory of this confession
gone, a snowman's melted face, the green grass, frozen and brown.

We let him leave because we know that on this day, he prefers the company
of the dead and a plow cannot till the winter's field. We know the call is
loud—the rumbling of night stars, the dripping of icicles on an empty night.
The noise of the dead doesn't make him swat at his ears; he turns
his hearing aids up. At home, he moves from window to window
and draws the shades to keep the moon's face from judgment. He searches
the corners of the house for that fuzzy spot of light from where
she will step out and come to him.

Cryogenics

Perry S. Nicholas

My mother stored her memories in a box
looking something like a cooler
for ten years after her husband died.

She put on a widow's black uniform,
walked wounded through the world,
but twice a day, once upon waking

and once before pill-induced sleep,
she knelt in front of it, popped
the lid open, and prayed to the past.

She transported them to Niagara Falls,
the Washington Monument, Disney World,
but never re-visited her young abused years

on the isolated island. The only life she allowed
herself to remember was the married one here—
two boys, one man, one kitchen, a driveway

full of work trucks. The cooler housed
her married years from nineteen to his death.
Then for a preserved decade she peeked inside.

Biophosphorescence

C E O'Rourke

Images in a dark sea
luminous flowers swaying, dancing
comb jellies and brittlestars
undulate in the light
look up now

I am a constellation
Pyxis Nautica
showing the way home

Here on the X-ray bed
dark fears worry
black spots on my bones
I try to envision health
try not to *see*
look up

White ceiling tiles
dark pinhole patterns
like scars from old memos:
"X-ray, bed 32"
a universe in reverse:
black stars in a white sky
find the celestial fix

I try to erase
the negative image
find the lodestar
look

Staring up I know
that when these stars fade
I will simply light the ceiling
or the night sky

be the fire
that warms you
the photons
lighting up your bones

Kathleen Gunton ~ *Golden Poppy*

Dread

Ronald Ruskin

The four of us were put together, alphabetically, two on either side of the cadaver.

> *Adler, Benjamin, Israel;*
>
> *Basso, Franco [Francesco];*
>
> *Berg, Lisa, Miriam;*
>
> *Callaghan, Ryan, Michael*

I stood at the head of our table and slowly unrolled the white shroud from the cadaver. A man lay flat and stiff on the table, his skin darkened, thick, and tight about his joints so that his knees and elbows seemed unnaturally polished and large. His skin was flaked in places and had the colour of orange rust. His feet were wrapped neatly in plastic bags tied over his ankles; his hands were similarly wrapped. The head which we could see now, although the plastic was translucent, revealed a face and shut eyes that appeared smoky, the jaw and brow sunken, the flesh ridged from possibly lying too much on one side. The features remained indistinct and smudged. Callaghan and I had anatomy lockers in the basement where we changed into our lab coats. We had bought our Grant's anatomy atlas and our text and we had purchased an anatomy kit—a wooden box of dissecting scalpels with replaceable blades, a dull metal probe, metal forceps, and some scissors in various shapes and sizes.

"Shall I take the plastic bag off the head?" I asked an anatomy demonstrator.

"That will be unnecessary. You will start dissection on the axillary fossa."

The axillary fossa? I checked my Grant's anatomy—it was the armpit. That was where we were to begin. At first there was Callaghan and I, one on each side of the cadaver. The next day we were joined by a rosy-cheeked stocky fellow with thick curly coal-black hair and immense expressive brown eyes whose family emigrated to Canada from Calabria when he was eight; his name was Francesco Basso, we called him Franco. He sang Italian opera and was a prankster. Franco had a room on the second floor of my residence. That first week we added a fourth partner, Lisa Berg; she had flaxen hair and blue pastel eyes and walked straighter than a statue. She was pretty in a boyish way and Jewish like me. She had a younger brother with Crohn's disease. She told us she felt anxious about being around cadavers. We named our cadaver Clive.

*   *   *

During the first week Lisa developed shortness of breath. Her heart "twisted" in her chest. When we lifted the white sheet off Clive and started dissection, Lisa confessed her period hadn't come.

"Yeah, well I'm going to be the first man to have twins," Franco chuckled.

"*Please,*" Lisa said. "I'm not pregnant—I'm not having sex with anyone."

Callaghan put down his scalpel. "I'm not feeling well. I've had dizzy spells. My neck has been stiff. I've had headaches for two weeks."

The smile disappeared from Franco's face. "*Headaches,* you said?"

"The pain comes and goes," Callaghan said. "It's getting worse."

"I have had headaches for weeks," Franco said.

"Meningitis—it could be meningitis." I said.

*   *   *

I covered Clive up with the white sheet. We leaned over him. I whispered. "Clive might have a lethal infection. I don't know where he got it or how it is spreading or where it is coming from, but I feel sick. I think that the infection must have killed him."

"You have symptoms?" Franco asked.

"Stomach pain," I said, "on the right side."

"That's your liver," Lisa said. "You have other symptoms?"

"Burning on the right side," I said. "Which side is the appendix on?"

"It's on the right side in most people," Callaghan said, "unless all your organs are reversed. Then it's on the left side and your heart is on the right side."

*   *   *

That afternoon I went to the campus doctor. I didn't tell him about my spider fear. I had this crazy fear there was a huge spider under my bed. Each night I had to check the sheets, the closet, and the mattress, to make sure there was no spider. I had been doing this for years. I had this fear since I was a little kid.

The doctor listened to my heart and lungs. He took my blood and urine for testing.

*   *   *

Franco confessed to me that he was losing hair. I had dreams my teeth were falling out. At night I lay in bed and heard my heart pounding in my chest. The blood swooshed in my ears. I wanted my heart to stop so I could get some peace and quiet, but then my life would be over.

We were all dying. There was no way around it.

The question was how soon death would come and would it be fast or slow? Would it be agonizing or painless, would it come when we were awake or at night when we were asleep? We huddled over Clive and shared our symptoms—the terror of heart disease, the panic of brain tumors, meningitis, hair loss, multiple sclerosis, the fear of Hodgkin's disease, or a bruise which might blossom overnight on our skin.

*   *   *

The no-man's zone between our patients and ourselves had fallen away. We merged with death in classes, in labs, in the hospitals.

I lied that I was fine. To tell the truth, I was lost in class. One of the senior med students, Stewart McRae, ran with Trevor Fairfax each morning along King Street, first one way and then the other. Trevor was training for the rugby team. Stewart was in the naval reserve and a long-distance runner for varsity. His dad was a big-shot surgeon and rear admiral in the Canadian Navy. I put on my sneakers and joined them. They were faster than me and in fantastic shape. I fell back and found my own route. After a while, though, I was almost able to keep up with them. I ran with them west past the Kingston Penitentiary to the Dupont plant and the golf club. On the way back we ran in the opposite direction along King Street to Causeway Bridge as far east as Fort Henry. It was murder running up the incline to the top of the fort. I kept my head down and didn't look up until I reached the summit. There you could see all of Kingston, RMC, the bridge, HMCS Cataraqui, the churches, and the lake, and these old Martello towers, which protected Kingston from the Americans during the war of 1812.

By the time I showered I was a new man.

*   *   *

In the second month of class, Callaghan found the answer we were searching for. It was in a psychiatric text that described a condition in medical students who believed they were experiencing the disease under study—a form of hypochondria. Nothing was written about the disorder, yet all my classmates suffered from it.

Like Clive and formaldehyde, the condition lingered all that year in medical school.

The Hug

Bruce Bennett

Her hair was black; she looked young and alive.
I knew that what she needed was a hug
and gave it to her. We just stood there hugging.
I didn't try to ask her any questions.
I seemed to feel her presence was enough.
It felt so good! I'd never dreamed about her,
and it's been years. So, that was all there was.
I know it sounds too simple when I say it,
but afterwards, you know, when I woke up
and thought about it, how she looked and felt,
it was like I had somehow solved the puzzle.
We'd all been searching, wondering all that time,
perplexed and angry: *Why? How could she do it?*
She did it. What she needed was a hug.

Reincarnation at the Kmart Intersection

Sarah Jefferis

I'm late to meet the doctor
and in the other lane
someone's grandpa tries to catch the light
and flips off his motorcycle,

rolls like a deer in the road.
Swerve around his red helmet,
think of another old man,
five years before at the same intersection,

how that bus driver stepped on the vertebrae
of the light, and gave it all up
on the steering wheel of his number 30.
Witnesses hard as ticks. No one willing

to find a pulse. Think
of the driver not hunched over,
but waltzing on dotted lines with a partner.
He's trying to find someone

to share the salt with.
But I am on my way to make you, little risotto,
and I am late, and my eggs are only good
for a few more hours.

In my rearview, I see two green Ford trucks,
old ones, almost hit this grandpa,
and I think, stop
your car, you know how to find

the pulse, count the tango beats,
you know the breaths one needs
to keep the glaciers from melting,
the bees from dying, the levees

from dropping their lace like the slip
of the first woman you loved. That woman
who always said *I didn't mean to*
the morning after she had.

How she said this every Sunday
before church. Stop the car,
that's the priest you loved as a child,
still as fox. Be the Samaritan

your mother rehearsed in you.
Surely others will stop, others who fuck
on kitchen tables without once thinking.
Stop the car,

that was your specter of a father on the cycle,
the one who could become a grandfather,
the one who rides Harleys
through Florida everglades.

I swear I saw you,
my little risotto, standing
between bus driver
and motorcycle man,

a hand in each,
them swinging you high.
I knew then how one cannot make one
if you pass by another.

Pamela Ferris-Olson ~ *The Winter Hour*

Contributors

Carolyn Agee is an actress and internationally published author living in the Pacific Northwest. Her recent and forthcoming credits include *Petrichor Machine*, *Perspectives Magazine*, and *A Flame in the Dark Quarterly*. Her website can be found at http://www.facebook.com/CarolynAgee.

Joan Applebaum is a teaching artist who has exhibited her work throughout New York State. She is also the Arts Studio Coordinator at the East Area Family YMCA and has taught in other programs including Partners for Arts Education and Kids in Art at SUNY Upstate Medical University. You can view other samples of her artwork at www.windyhillstudioarts.com.

Jackie Bartley's poems have appeared most recently in *Nimrod, Southern Humanities Review,* and *sou'wester*. Her second poetry collection, *Ordinary Time*, won the 2006 Spire Press Poetry Prize.

Susan M. Behuniak is a professor and Chair of Political Science at Le Moyne College. Her teaching and publications lie at the intersection of law, politics, and medicine. Much of what she has learned about end-of-life issues comes from her volunteer work with hospice patients and their loved ones.

Bruce Bennett's most recent chapbooks are a letterpress edition of his rhymed fables, *The Bestial Floor* (Wells College Press), and a sonnet sequence, *A Girl Like You* (Finishing Line Press). He is a professor and Chair of English at Wells College, where he also directs the creative writing program. He is very pleased to have his work included again in *The Healing Muse*.

Nina Bennett is the author of *Forgotten Tears: A Grandmother's Journey Through Grief*. Her poetry has appeared in journals including *Alehouse, Panache, Yale Journal for Humanities in Medicine, The Broadkill Review*, and anthologies such as *Spaces Between Us: Poetry, Prose, and Art on HIV/AIDS*.

Linda Bigness is an internationally exhibited artist who resides in Central New York. Her work has been exhibited in several prestigious solo and group shows that have involved notable jurors such as art critic Clement Greenberg, Ivan Karp, OK Harris Gallery, NYC, and Tom Piche, Director, The Daum Museum of Contemporary Art.

Jennifer Campbell is an English professor in Buffalo, New York, and a co-editor of *Earth's Daughters and Beyond Bones*. Her book of poetry, *Driving Straight Through*, was published by FootHills in 2008. Recent work appears in *Eclipse, Slipstream, Rockhurst Review, PRECIPICe*, and *Slant*. Work is forthcoming in *Saranac Review* and *New Millennium Writings*.

Elizabeth Carey, born in Portland, Oregon, majored in urban studies and political science at Columbia University. Love for running, coaching, nature, and family inspires her writing. Currently a student at Syracuse University's S.I. Newhouse School of Public Communications, she is earning a master's degree in Magazine, Newspaper and Online Journalism.

Joan Cofrancesco's work has appeared in *Kalliope, Sinister Wisdom, Howling Dog, Bay Windows, Point Judith Point, Womanspirit, 13th Moon, Lake Effect, Amazon Quarterly, Silverman Review, The Healing Muse, Many Waters, The Harvard Gay and Lesbian Review, Potato Eyes*, and other literary magazines. Her poetry books include *Walpurgis Night*, 1993, *Cat Bones in the Tree*, 1998, and *Kerouac's Cat*, and 2006.

Hannah Craig lives in Pittsburgh, Pennsylvania. Her work has recently appeared in *Fence, Post Road*, the *Norton Anthology of Hint Fiction*, and elsewhere. She is an assistant editor for *Anti-Poetry Magazine*.

Elinor Cramer's first poetry collection, *She Is a Pupa, Soft and White* will be published by Word Press in December 2011. Her poems have also appeared in *Stone Canoe* and *The Comstock Review*. Elinor lives in Syracuse, New York, where she practices psychotherapy.

Barbara Crooker's books are *Radiance*, winner of the 2005 Word Press First Book Award, *Line Dance* (Word Press, 2008), winner of the 2009 Paterson Award for Excellence in Literature, and *More* (C&R Press, 2010). Her work has also appeared on *Verse Daily* and been read by Garrison Keillor on *The Writer's Almanac*.

Lois Dorschel is secretary for the Center for Bioethics and Humanities at SUNY Upstate Medical University and managing editor of *The Healing Muse*. She enjoys retreating to her cabin in the woods with her husband Marty, gardening, sharing life with her family, and receiving unconditional love from her Labrador, Chloe.

Stephanie Elliott has been published in *Confrontation* and *Promethean*. She holds a bachelor's in literature from the City College of New York, and has recently completed a memoir, *The Moon to Swallow*, about her experience with brain injury caused by the medications used to treat an existing illness. She is currently working on a novel.

Donna Emerson's recent publications include *The Place That Inhabits Us: Poems of the San Francisco Bay Watershed, Phoebe, Eclipse*, among others. She won the 2010 *Tiny Light* Flash competition. Chapbooks include *This Water, Body*

Rhymes, nominated for the California Book Award, and the forthcoming *Wild Mercy.* She lives in Petaluma, California.

Pamela Ferris-Olson, an award-winning photographer, is a keen observer of life, water and light. Her book *Living in the Heartland: Three Extraordinary Women's Stories* was published in 2010. Pam is currently pursuing her doctorate in Leadership and Change.

Clifford Paul Fetters has poems published in *Oxford American, Poetry East, Appalachia, The New York Review of Books, The Seattle Review, OnEarth, The Willow Review, 5AM, Rattle, Light*, and others. He lives in Florida with his wife, novelist Debra Dean.

June Frankland Baker was born in Upstate New York and taught in high schools in both North Syracuse and Skaneateles before she moved to the West. Her poems have appeared for thirty years in literary journals and anthologies, including *The Blueline Anthology* published by Syracuse University Press in 2004.

Amy L. Friedman, MD, professor of surgery, is the Director of Transplantation at SUNY Upstate Medical University. Trained at Princeton, SUNY Downstate, and the University of Pennsylvania, she previously served on the faculties of Penn and Yale Universities. She is a member of the American Society of Transplant Surgeons, and is secretary of the American Association of Kidney Patients. Her immediate family includes two transplant recipients and one live donor.

M. Frost, a former large-animal veterinarian, currently studies environmental health. She serves as editor of *The Stew*, a literary and arts magazine published through the Johns Hopkins Bloomberg School of Public Health. She has published a chapbook, *Cow Poetry* (Finishing Line Press), and poems in numerous journals, including *The Healing Muse*.

Angela M. Giles Patel lives in Norfolk, Massachusetts. In addition to working on a collection of poetry, she is writing a book which explores the unkind quiet that emerges after the death of a sibling. This is her first publication.

Sriharsha Gowtham is a second year medical student at SUNY Upstate Medical University. Art in medicine is a passion of Sriharsha, not only for the sake of learning anatomy, but also for the appreciation of the textures, pencil strokes, and shadows. It is a relaxing pastime for him.

Kathleen Gunton lives in Orange, California. While working on a memoir of her convent days, she continues to publish prose, poetry, and photography. Recent work has appeared in *The Los Angeles Review, Off The Coast, Thema, Inkwell*, and *Shenandoah*. Her work has found a home at *The Healing Muse* since 2005.

Amy Haddad teaches ethics at Creighton University where she is Director of the Center for Health Policy and Ethics. Her poetry has been published in *American Journal of Nursing, Reflections, Journal of General Internal Medicine, Journal of*

Medical Humanities, and *Touch*.

Diane Halsted edits, writes, and teaches classes in writing poetry, creative nonfiction, and memoir to older learners in San Luis Obispo, California. She was a college English teacher for twenty-five years. When she isn't teaching or writing, she is riding her horse, gardening, or traveling.

Today, **Jenny Haust** is a full time mother. After the birth of her first son, Jenny pursued her MBA degree from Syracuse University, and graduated in 2007. Jenny currently resides in Upstate New York with her husband, two young boys, and their beagle, Maude Lilly.

Jennifer Heatley lives in Ithaca, New York where she is a school social worker. She is currently working on her first blog, "A Single Feather." In her spare time she enjoys the simple pleasures of life with her partner, dogs, chickens, and flowers. This is her first published poem, written for Margaret Launius.

Karen Holmberg writes poetry and nonfiction that has appeared or is forthcoming in such magazines as *Quarterly West, Southern Poetry Review, West Branch, Cave Wall, Potomac Review, Black Warrior Review, New Madrid, Poetry East,* and *Cimarron Review*. She teaches in the MFA program at Oregon State University.

Joyce Holmes McAllister is retired after thirty years at Cornell University as a Registrar and is happily pursuing her first love, poetry. She has been published on *Gratefulness.org* and in *The Comstock Review*, as well as in local newsletters and newspapers. She is delighted to have her work appear again in *The Healing Muse*.

Gail Hosking is the author of *Snake's Daughter: The Roads in and Out of War* published by the University of Iowa Press. Her poems and essays have appeared in such places as *The Florida Review, The New Jersey Star Ledger*, and *Nimrod International*. She holds an MFA from Bennington College and teaches creative writing at Rochester Institute of Technology.

Katharyn Howd Machan's poems have appeared in numerous magazines, anthologies, and textbooks, including *The Bedford Introduction to Literature*, and in thirty collections, most recently *Belly Words: Poems of Dance* (Split Oak Press, 2009). She is a professor in the Department of Writing at Ithaca College in central New York.

Andrea Hsue grew up cradled by Binghamton, New York's comforting, rolling hills and under its brooding, cloudy skies. Her journey continues as she begins internship in Providence, Rhode Island. She loves, among many things, deep movements of the heart, the beauty of shared tears of joy or sadness, and the unnatural pursuit of meekness.

Saratoga Springs visual artist and poet **Mary Kathryn Jablonski** freelances in design and public relations. She is the author of the chapbook *To the Husband I Have Not Yet Met*, and her poems have appeared in numerous literary journals including the *Beloit Poetry Journal, Salmagundi*, and *Blueline*.

Sarah Jefferis' first book of poetry, *Forgetting the Salt*, was published in 2008 (Foothills Press). Her poems have appeared in *The Mississippi Review, The Hollins Critic, The Healing Muse, Icon, The Patterson Review* and other journals. She lives and writes in Ithaca, New York, with her partner and their two daughters.

Karen Kozicki is a fine art photographer, working predominantly in black and white and black and white infrared. Her work has been shown in numerous juried shows, including Schweinfurth Memorial Art Gallery's *Made in New York*, in Auburn, New York, and Cooperstown Art Association's National Exhibition, where she received a Purchase Prize in 2010.

Susan J. Levy, M.Ed., LMFT, has been a psychotherapist in private practice for almost thirty years working with individuals, couples, families, and groups. She specializes in health and wellness, chronic illness, grief, and bereavement. Susan recently completed her certification as a Community Practitioner of Integral Qigong.

V. P. Loggins is the author of *The Fourth Paradise* and *Heaven Changes*. His work has appeared in *Aethlon, The Baltimore Review, Cæsura, Memoir* (and), *Poet Lore* and *The Southern Review*, among others. A finalist for the 2011 May Swenson Award, he teaches at the United States Naval Academy.

James M. Loiselle was born in 1986 in Hammond, Louisiana. He grew up in Locke, New York and attended Southern Cayuga Schools in Poplar Ridge, New York. He can do anything with any of the functions of a digital camera, enjoying the different and unexpected results. Currently he lives in Kenner, Louisiana.

Susannah Loiselle and her family live near Locke, New York. She received a certificate for Fiction Writing from the DWC PRO program of the YMCA in Syracuse in 2010 and is currently working on a novel. Her poetry chapbook, *God Speaks to me at the Salvation Army Thrift Store*, was published in 2004. She enjoys writing, watercolors & drawing, and photography.

Linda Loomis teaches creative writing at SUNY Oswego, where she was previously director of journalism and editor of the alumni magazine. While editor of *The Review*, then a weekly newspaper in Liverpool, she was named New York Press Association writer of the year. She and her four grandchildren enjoy reading and writing together.

J.P. Maney is a graduate of the Iowa Writers' Workshop. His work has appeared in *Western Humanities Review, Green Mountains Review, The Bridge, Confrontation, Troika*, and many others. He has edited four anthologies, including *Sudden Fiction, Sudden Fiction International*, and *A Celestial Omnibus: Short Fiction on Faith*. He lives near Cooperstown, in the foothills of the Catskill Mountains.

David C. Manfredi grew up in New York City and attended the University of

Bologna Medical School. Poetry has always been a part of his life and his experiences frame his writing. He views himself as a poet who makes his living as a physician, and defines a good poem as one he would read again.

Twice nominated for the Pushcart Prize, **Suzanne McConnell**'s work has appeared in *The Huffington Post, The Saint Ann's Review, The Fiddlehead*, and elsewhere. An excerpt from her recently completed first novel won second prize in So to Speak's 2008 contest. She teaches at Hunter College and at hospitals, and is Fiction Editor at the *Bellevue Literary Review*.

Kailyn McCord is thrilled to appear in *The Healing Muse*. Her work has previously appeared in *The Believer, Reed College Creative Review, The 826 Quarterly*, and online at *The Rumpus*. Kailyn eats, sleeps, writes, and works behind the scenes in Portland, Oregon.

Antara Mitra was born and raised in India, which inspires her fiction. She is currently pursuing her MPH. Antara's writings have been published in *The Statesman, The Post-Standard, Herb Companion* and *British Airways News*. She loves traveling with her family.

Barbara Nevaldine is a graduate of Syracuse University and currently employed as a research associate in the Department of Radiation Oncology at SUNY Upstate Medical University. She is a member of the Syracuse Camera Club and the Beaver Lake photo group. Her hobbies are gardening and photography.

Perry S. Nicholas is an assistant professor of English at Erie Community College North in Buffalo, New York. His poems have appeared in *Hudson View, Word Worth, Feile-Festa, Louisiana Literature, Chautauqua Literary Journal*, and one is forthcoming in *The New York Quarterly*. His book, *The River of You*, was published in September 2009 by FootHills Publishing.

Heidi Nightengale lives, works, and writes in the Finger Lakes region of Central New York. She teaches for the SUNY Empire State College. Her work has appeared in regional and national literary journals. Her chapbook, *Bird Vision*, was published by Pudding House Press in 2009.

Zofia Nowicki is an artist and radiologist in Scottsdale, Arizona. She grew up in an artistic and medical family and has studied art in Florida and Italy. While in medical school, Zofia completed a series about the patient and doctor relationship. She works primarily in oils on canvas, with portraits being her favorite subject. Having recently moved to Arizona, Zofia is currently exploring the western landscape. www.artzofia.com.

Basilia Nwankwo is a third-year medical student at SUNY Upstate Medical University who is interested in global health and health disparities, as well as a lifelong student of the arts and creative works.

Laurie Oot Leonard, BSN, is a chemical dependency nurse at Crouse Hospital in Syracuse, New York. Her passions include growing beautiful gardens and creating quilt/fiber art. She has been writing since Mrs. Sidmore's fourth grade class.

Charlotte F. Otten's poems have appeared in *Southern Humanities Review, Christian Science Monitor*, and *Darkling*. She recently read her poems from *Quiddity* on NPR in Springfield, Illinois. She is the editor of *The Book of Birth Poetry* (Virago/Bantam), of English Women's Voices 1540-1700 (University Press of Florida), and *A Lycanthropy Reader* (Syracuse University Press).

C E O'Rourke is an award winning essayist and poet. First published at eleven years of age, Ceo follows a long line of writers/artists from the Campbell-Nairn clan. Aside from researching, Ceo can be found backpacking in our spectacular North American wilderness. Recent publishers include McGraw-Hill and Portal Literary Magazine.

Fani Papageorgiou was born in Athens. Her poems have appeared in magazines and literary journals in the US (*The New Republic, The South Carolina Review, Conjunctions* et al) where she was nominated for a Pushcart Prize, in the UK (*Poetry Review, Magma* et al) where she was a finalist for the 2009 MsLexia Women's Poetry Competition, and in Australia.

Tish Pearlman is currently host/producer of an award-winning public radio interview show called "Out of Bounds." In June 2009 Pearlman underwent openheart surgery. This experience prompted her to write poetry for the first time in twenty years. The complete collection about her heart surgery experience, *The Fix Is In* (Finishing Line Press, 2011), is available this November. She lives in Ithaca, New York.

Simon Perchik is an attorney whose poems have appeared in *Partisan Review, The New Yorker,* and elsewhere. For more information, including his essay *Magic, Illusion and Other Realities*, and a complete bibliography, please visit his website at www.simonperchik.com.

David Plumb's writing has appeared in *The Washington Post, Sport Literate, Wellness and Writing, The Miami Herald*, and the *Homeless Not Helpless Anthology*. The author of nine books, a Syracuse University graduate and once an orderly at Syracuse Memorial Hospital, he teaches English at Broward College in Florida.

Dr. W. Soyini Powell, a SUNY Upstate Medical University graduate is now director of Women's Services at a Philadelphia Catholic Hospital whose mission is to serve the poor and indigent. She has traveled to West and East Africa working with grassroots organizations in support of women's reproductive rights. *The Healing Muse* is a wonderful outlet for her creative voice.

Claudia Reder, the author of *My Father* and *Miro and Other Poems* (Bright Hill Press, 2001), was recently awarded first prize in the Charlotte Newberger Poetry Prize from Lilith Magazine. She teaches at California State University Channel Islands. Poems are forthcoming in *New Millenium Writings, Bridges: A Jewish*

Feminist Journal, and *Chiron Review*.

Oliver Rice's poems have appeared in journals and anthologies in the United States and abroad. His interview with *Creekwalker* was released by that zine in January, 2010. His book of poems, *On Consenting to be a Man*, is offered by Cyberwit, in Allahabad, India, and on Amazon. His online chapbook, *Afterthoughts, Siestas*, and his recording of his *The Institute for Higher Study*, appeared in *Mudlark* in December 2010.

Ronald Ruskin, MD, is a psychiatrist at Mount Sinai Hospital in Toronto and an editor and co-founder of *Ars Medica*, a journal of medicine, the arts, and humanities. His narratives have appeared in *JAMA, American Journal of Psychiatry, CMAJ, Queen's Quarterly,* and *Parchment*. His medical thriller called *The Last Panic*, was published by Bantam in 1979.

Annita Sawyer is a clinical psychologist in practice thirty years. In 2003 she turned sixty and began writing. She has been to Bread Loaf, Phillip Lopate's workshop at Skidmore, Ragdale, Vermont Studio Center, and VCCA. Her work has appeared in *The Healing Muse, The MacGuffin, The Saint Ann's Review,* and others. This essay is from her memoir, *SMOKING CIGARETTES, EATING GLASS*.

Patricia Seitz's paintings are distinctive for their bold and simple brush strokes. She gravitates towards luminescent light and triadic color choices. She is an active member in Oil Painters of America, Plein Air Painters of CNY, Central New York Art Guild, Fingerlakes Artists and Crafters, Artist BlueBooks of North America, and Ask Art.

Johanna Shapiro is the director of the Program in Medical Humanities and Arts at the University of California Irvine, School of Medicine. She is a poetry co-editor for the online journal *Pulse: Voices from the Heart of Medicine* and has published original poetry in a wide variety of medical journals.

Christopher Stark Biddle is a writer who lives in Craftsbury Common, Vermont. He has worked on the problems of social and economic development in Africa, Asia, and Central Europe, and is the author of numerous studies and articles on civil society. Stark has studied at the Wildbranch Writer's Workshop and the Breadloaf Writer's Conference.

Craig W. Steele is a writer and university biologist who lives in the urban countryside of northwestern Pennsylvania. His poetry has appeared recently or is forthcoming in *The Yale Journal for Humanities in Medicine, Perspectives Magazine, Yale Anglers' Journal, WestWard Quarterly, The Lyric*, and elsewhere.

Howard F. Stein, Ph.D., a medical and psychoanalytic anthropologist, is professor and Special Assistant to the Chair in the Department of Family and Preventive Medicine, University of Oklahoma Health Sciences Center, Oklahoma City, Oklahoma. He has published six books and chapbooks of poetry; the most recent is *Seeing Rightly with the Heart* (November 2010). In 2006 he was nominated for

Oklahoma Poet Laureate.

Teresa Sutton of Poughkeepsie, New York, teaches twelfth grade English at Roy C. Ketcham High School in Wappingers Falls, New York, and adjuncts in the graduate education department at Marist College. She has a master's degree in education and an MFA in poetry. She is a mother of two.

Esperanza Tielbaard, Colombian, attended the Conservatorio Antonio Maria Valencia of Fine Arts in Cali, Colombia. An active multi-disciplinary fine artist, she is passionate about color and texture. She employs diverse materials such as bone, silk, wood, metals and glass to produce artwork that has meaning beyond simple, decorative values. The work "Energize" is inspiration and motivation to get a walk to spiritual energy from the tranquil natural world.

Yolanda Tooley fell in love with 35mm film/darkroom photography over thirty years ago. Her studio in Brewerton, New York overlooking Oneida Lake, gives her much inspiration and solace. She has shown her work in national juried shows, and her photographs are published in many arts journals and anthologies. She is honored to be included again in *The Healing Muse*.

Jack Tourin was born in Poughkeepsie, New York. During World War II, he served in the U.S. Navy on the island of Guam, and his wife Beatrice, was an Army nurse in Burma. After the war, he attended USC in Los Angeles. For many years, he taught school in Indiana. He has written memoirs, poetry, short stories, and a novel. Jack and his wife live in California.

Zin Min Tun is a fourth-year medical student at SUNY Upstate Medical University. Zin was born in Burma, and when he was sixteen, his father won a DV (Diversity Visa) lottery, which granted an opportunity for Zin's family to come to United States as permanent residents. He graduated from UC Berkeley, California, with a bachelor's degree with honors in chemical biology, and will graduate from Upstate in May 2012.

Pediatrician **Kelley White** has worked in inner-city and rural settings. Her poems have appeared in journals including *Exquisite Corpse, Rattle* and *JAMA*. Her most recent books are *Toxic Environment* (Boston Poet Press) and *Two Birds in a Flame* (Beech River Books). She received a 2008 PCA grant.

Valerie Wohlfeld's most recent book of poetry is *Woman with Wing Removed* (Truman State University Press, 2010). Her first collection, *Thinking the World Visible*, won the Yale Younger Poets Prize (Yale University Press, 1994). She holds an MFA from Vermont College.

Kathleen Gunton ~ *The Calm*

Acknowledgments

The following people have generously donated money to this issue of *The Healing Muse*. We are deeply grateful for their support.

Linda Albert   Felice Aull   Kim Babcock

Consortium for Culture and Medicine   Cynthia Bailey & Kathy Young

Sheree Lyn Batson   Karen Blank   Rosemarie Cittadino

Wendy Edwards   Cynthia Garrett   Nancy Geyer

Thomas Gibbs   Shelley Gilroy   Michael & Wendy Gordon

Judith Hannan   Anthony Italiano   Margaret Johnston

Joyce Holmes McAllister   David Manfredi   Sandra McCabe

Deirdre Neilen   Gloria Neilen   Janice Nelson   Patricia Numann

Joel Potash & Sandra Hurd   Marsha Pross   Christine Ryan

Suzanne Schaff   Meghan Scott   Johanna Shapiro

Gloria Sheehan   Sharon Smith   Jane & Christopher St. Andrews

Joann Tapley   Delia Temes   Lois Trumbull

Cindy Wojtecki   Carolyn Zaroff

and an Anonymous Annual Supporter!

Support *The Healing Muse*

We provide a forum for artistic approaches to the body, illness, and medicine by publishing the voices and perspectives of people with illness and disability, health care practitioners, and caregivers. All donors will be acknowledged in the next issue.

$50 (Contributor) — $100 (Sponsor) — $500 (Benefactor)
Each donation receives two complimentary copies of the current issue.

All contributions are tax deductible.
Please make checks payable to
The Healing Muse.

The Healing Muse
Center for Bioethics and Humanities
SUNY Upstate Medical University
618 Irving Avenue
Syracuse, NY 13210

www.thehealingmuse.org

Order Your Copies Now!

		Quantity	Amount
The Healing Muse, Volume 11	$10.00	_____	$ _____
Individual Back Issues			
Volumes 1-5, 7-10 (indicate volume)	$7.50	_____	$ _____
Discount Package (Volumes 1-5, 7-11)	$77.50	_____	$ _____
Three-year Subscription			
(starts with current year)	$25.00	_____	$ _____
Educators' Discount on back issues			
(15+ copies)	$5.00	_____	$ _____
Postage: If *outside* U.S., add $3.00/issue	$3.00	_____	$ _____
Support The Healing Muse — Donations			$ _____
(tax deductible)			
	TOTAL		$ _____

Please send a check or money order made out to The Healing Muse.

Send orders to:

The Healing Muse
Center for Bioethics and Humanities
SUNY Upstate Medical University
618 Irving Avenue
Syracuse, NY 13210

Mail to:

Name   _____

Address   _____

                  _____

Email address: _____

For additional order forms, visit our website at: **www.thehealingmuse.org**

Submission Guidelines & Editorial Policy for *The Healing Muse*

Submissions are collected and juried from September 1st through May 1st. The editors try to respond to submissions within three months' time (with the exception of the visual art submissions. These are selected after June 1st). **The maximum length of text is 2,500 words (typed double-spaced).** Poetry need not be double-spaced.

We recommend that you read excerpts from one or two issues before you submit your manuscript. You will find these on our website: www.thehealingmuse.org

All submissions should be sent to:

The Healing Muse
SUNY Upstate Medical University
Center for Bioethics and Humanities
618 Irving Ave
Syracuse, NY 13210

• Authors are asked to submit hard copy manuscripts and SASE for return of original manuscripts. Please put the word count on the first page. We ask authors whose work is selected for publication to email us their work as an electronic Word file, to identify their submission as *fiction*, *non-fiction*, or *poetry*, and to enclose a three-line bio (*fifty words maximum*) for our Contributors' page.

• Visual artists should submit clear originals, slides, or an electronic file at 300 dpi. Most of the artwork published is printed in black and white, so please take this into account when submitting your work. All original artwork, slides, photographs, and disks will be returned to the author. Please include SASE with your submission.

• Manuscripts and artworks are considered with the understanding that they have not been published previously in print or electronic format (including the Internet). We ask authors whose work is accepted to sign a statement declaring that their work has not been previously published by them or under another name. The editors screen submissions carefully for plagiarism.

- Accepted manuscripts are edited and returned to authors for approval.

- **Confidentiality**. The privacy of patients and clients of health care practitioners should be protected. Physicians and health care practitioners who write about their patients must alter identifying details and characteristics.

- Contributors will receive two copies of each issue in which their work appears; additional copies are available at a reduced rate.

Questions? Please e-mail us at *The Healing Muse:* **hlgmuse@upstate.edu**

Or visit us at: **www.thehealingmuse.org**

Readers' and Educators' Guides

➤ Looking for ideas on how to use stories, poems, essays, and visual arts from *The Healing Muse* as a text in a classroom?

➤ Interested in *The Muse* for your book group?

➤ Perhaps you're just looking for a way to process the wealth of experiences and perspectives represented in *The Muse*?

Here are a few excerpts from the Readers' Guide for this issue of *The Muse*:

1. In Elizabeth Carey's "The Waiting Room," the narrator says:

   Thank god for the straight-shooting hospice nurse. With her black bob motionless atop her petite, plump frame, she put it to me. The force of her words pushed me back against the fridge and I slumped to the floor. She put it to us, my mom and me, to be the ones to care for him; to help him go; to let him be; to push his ice flow into a cold, dark sea, to leave this wretched world and beautiful compassion and all the flighty antelope and sneaky cougars behind.

   How is it that the narrator can be grateful for bad news told with such force? Discuss what you think the hospice nurse is communicating to the narrator and her mother. How would you want to be told bad news? How would you break it to a family, if you were the hospice nurse?

2. Amy Friedman's "I Killed a Man with My Own Two Hands" is a confession of guilt that is almost brutal in its self-condemnation. At the same time, it engages the reader's empathy and raises the question of understanding and forgiveness. How do you judge the narrator's actions from the point of view of a doctor or medical student? From the point of view of a patient? If these views are different, should they be?

3. How does Elinor Cramer's poem, "Mrs. Bean Fighting Mad at Me," raise questions about the independence, or, in ethical terms, autonomy, of those who lose cognitive function as they age? What are the ethical and emotional quandaries involved with caring for those who lose cognitive function?

4. What does Barbara Crooker's poem "February Second" tell us about grief and those who do not cease to mourn?

Find **Readers' and Educators' Guides**
for this and other issues of *The Healing Muse* at our website

www.thehealingmuse.org

Read Our Blog
Join Our Mailing List

All the information you need is now located on one page!

www.thehealingmusecafe.blogspot.com/